The Seeker's Guide
to the Christian Story

Other books by Mitch Finley

Building Christian Families (with Kathy Finley)

Your Family in Focus: Appreciating What You Have, Making It Even Better

The Seeker's Guide to Being Catholic

Everybody Has a Guardian Angel . . . And Other Lasting Lessons I Learned in Catholic Schools

Heavenly Helpers: St. Anthony and St. Jude

Whispers of Love: Encounters with Deceased Relatives and Friends

Catholic Is Wonderful

The Joy of Being Catholic

101 Ways to Nourish Your Soul

Let's Begin with Prayer: 130 Prayers for Junior and Senior High Schools

Surprising Mary: Meditations and Prayers on the Mother of Jesus

The Seeker's Guide to the Christian Story

MITCH FINLEY

WITHDRAWN

Seeker Series
Loyola Press

CHICAGO

Originally published as *Time Capsules of the Church*
© 1990 Our Sunday Visitor

©1998 Mitch Finley
Printed in the United States of America

Loyola Press
3441 North Ashland Avenue
Chicago, Illinois 60657
1-800-621-1008

The Seeker Series *from Loyola Press provides trustworthy guides for your journey of faith and is dedicated to the principle that asking questions is not only all right . . . it is essential.*

Cover and interior design: Shawn Biner
Cover photo courtesy of: ©North Carolina Museum of Art/Corbis

All quotations from Scripture are from the New Revised Standard Version Bible: Catholic Edition, Copyright 1993 and 1989, Division of Christian Education of the National Council of Churches of Christ in the United States of America.

Library of Congress Cataloging-in-Publication Data
Finley, Mitch.
    The seeker's guide to the Christian story / Mitch Finley.
        p.   cm. — (Seeker series)
    Includes bibliographical references (p.   ) and index.
    ISBN 0-8294-1020-1
    1. Catholic Church—History. 2. Church history.
I. Title.
II. Series: Seeker series (Chicago, Ill.)
BX945.2.F56   1998   97-46641
282'.09—dc21   CIP

1 2 3 4 5 / 01 00 99 98

To our three sons:
Sean Thomas, Patrick Daniel,
and Kevin Andrew.

When I want to understand
what is happening today
or try to decide
what will happen tomorrow,
I look back.
— *Oliver Wendell Holmes (1809–94)*

Contents

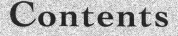

ACKNOWLEDGMENTS / ix

NOTE ON THE REVISED EDITION / xi

INTRODUCTION / xiii

CHAPTER 1
Jesus of Nazareth / 1

CHAPTER 2
The Early Church / 19

CHAPTER 3
The Church Gives Birth
to the New Testament / 41

CHAPTER 4
The Constantinian Era / 61

CHAPTER 5
The Council of Chalcedon / 81

CHAPTER 6
The Crusades, the Inquisition,
Saint Dominic, and Saint Francis
of Assisi / 101

CHAPTER 7
The Protestant Reformation / 119

CHAPTER 8
The Council of Trent / 139

CHAPTER 9
Ultramontanism and the
First Vatican Council / 165

CHAPTER 10
Pius X and the Modernist Crisis / 189

CHAPTER 11
John XXIII and the
Second Vatican Council / 215

EPILOGUE
The Current State of the Church / 239

NOTES / 247

INDEX / 259

Thanks to my wife, Kathy, and to our three sons, to whom this book is dedicated. Even if you hardly knew I was writing a book, your presence and love kept me going more often than you know.

A special thanks to Jeremy Langford of Loyola Press for believing in this book enough to publish a revised, expanded edition. It's good to know editors who want to publish books that people will read.

I am not a professional Church historian. Thanks, therefore, to those scholars upon whose shoulders I stand. Their work was indispensable to me in writing this book. I wish to acknowledge my dependence upon and recommend to readers the following works: *A Concise History of the Catholic Church,* Revised and Expanded Edition, by Thomas Bokenkotter (Doubleday Image Books, 1990); *How to Read Church History,* Vol. 1, "From the Beginnings to the Fifteenth Century," by Jean Comby (Crossroad, 1985); *The Beginnings of the Church,* by Frederick J. Cwiekowski (Paulist Press, 1988); *The First*

Seven Ecumenical Councils (325–787): Their History and Theology, by Leo Donald Davis, S.J. (Michael Glazier, 1987); *Church History: Twenty Centuries of Catholic Christianity,* by John C. Dwyer (Paulist Press, 1985); *The People of God Series,* by Anthony E. Gilles (St. Anthony Messenger Press, 1983–88); *Pope John XXIII: Shepherd of the Modern World,* by Peter Hebblethwaite (Doubleday, 1985); *A Short History of the Catholic Church,* by J. Derek Holmes and Bernard W. Bickers (Paulist Press, 1984); *A History of the Christian Tradition: From Its Jewish Origins to the Reformation,* by Thomas D. McGonigle and James F. Quigley (Paulist Press, 1988); *Pontiffs: Popes Who Shaped History,* by John Jay Hughes (Our Sunday Visitor, 1994); and *A Popular History of the Catholic Church,* by Carl Koch (Saint Mary's Press, 1997).

Finally, I wish to express my gratitude to Michael Leach, of the Crossroad Publishing Company, New York, for generously donating to the project of writing this book a complete set of the excellent ten-volume *History of the Church,* edited by Hubert Jedin (Crossroad, 1981–86). This set of books provided a constant source of detailed historical material upon which I was able to rely with complete confidence.

NOTE ON THE REVISED EDITION

This revised, updated edition incorporates new material, primarily in Chapter 6. Like its predecessor, it is designed to give the reader a "feel" for the story of the Roman Catholic Church without dumping a truckload of information on him or her. There is no shortage of other popular treatments of Church history to which the reader may turn for more complete information.

INTRODUCTION

To read history is to investigate the past. To read history is also to try to understand the present in the light of the past and to learn from that past in order to shape a better future. Therefore, one reads history to nourish wisdom and hope.

"The present state of things," said Samuel Johnson (1709–84), "is the consequence of the past; and it is natural to inquire as to the sources of the good we enjoy or the evils we suffer. If we act only for ourselves, to neglect the study of history is not prudent; if entrusted with the care of others, it is not just."

There are many perspectives on history, some positive, some not. The opinion of poet Henry Wadsworth Longfellow (1807–82) was both charming and pessimistic. He said: "The history of the past is a mere puppet show. A little man comes out and blows a little trumpet, and goes in again. You look for something new, and lo! another little man comes out and blows another little trumpet, and goes in again. And it is all over."

To give credit where it is due, however, perhaps Longfellow was only repeating what Qoheleth said centuries before: "What has been, that will be: what has been done, that will be done. Nothing is new under the sun" (Ecclesiastes 1:9).

When another nineteenth-century poet, Alfred Lord Tennyson (1806–82), thought about it, he planted both feet squarely on the side of a nostalgic view of the past: "So sad, so fresh, the days that are no more."

Well, maybe . . .

An ancient Greek philosopher, Marcus Tullius Cicero (106–43 B.C.), insisted that one must know history in order to become a mature person: "Not to know what has been transacted in former times is to be always a child. If no use is made of the labors of past ages, the world must remain always in the infancy of knowledge."

To focus specifically on the history of the Church, says Church historian Hubert Jedin, is to learn about "the growth in time and space of the Church founded by Christ."

There is more to Church history than that, however. One who would nourish an adult faith must pay attention to the history of the Church. For if I know where I come from, if I understand better the roots of my religious tradition, the "stories of the Church," I become liberated to face the present and the future with greater confidence, hope, and common sense.

To take a tip from Cicero, to overlook Church history is to remain spiritually a child. If I ignore the stories of Church history, in my own self, on a tiny scale, I must constantly struggle with issues and ideas that the Catholic community has probably faced many times down through the centuries. Why not take a lesson from the Church's nearly two thousand years of experience? Pope John XXIII, in the address with which he opened the Second Vatican Council in 1962 said, "History is the teacher of life."

The Word of God became a human being in the historical Jesus of Nazareth. This means that history, sacred or secular, has a religious dimension. "God has revealed himself to us in history by becoming man," wrote Thomas Merton (1915–68). "Christ, the Man-God, is the Lord of History. Awareness of Christ implies therefore some awareness of history. . . ."

Stories from the Church's past take seriously the conviction that Jesus of Nazareth constitutes the center of history. Frederick Buechner states it plainly and with a touch of wit: "The real turning point in human history is less apt to be the day the wheel is invented or Rome falls than the day a boy is born to a couple of hick Jews."

It is critical, of course, to not drive a mental wedge between secular and sacred history, as if they have nothing in common. "The evidence of history," declared the great Jesuit theologian Karl Rahner (1904–84), "shows that revolutionary phases in the past history of the Church coincided with revolutionary phases in the past history of secular society—indeed, that they even emerge from them."

How important is Church history? Philosopher Alfred North Whitehead (1861–1947) insisted that religious beliefs depend upon history and must not be separated from it. "Religions commit suicide," he cautioned, "when they find their inspiration in their dogmas. The inspiration of religion lies in the history of religion."

This book presents eleven essays on "moments" in Church history, the effects of which are still felt today by ordinary Catholics, as well as other Christians. These past events contribute much to the experience of today's people of God, the Church.

It is risky, of course, to isolate a given "moment" in Church history from what went before and what came after, but for the purposes of this book it must suffice to remind the reader that such is possible only for purposes of discussion. History is not a series of unrelated events but, one might say, an ongoing narrative. Each event in Church history is connected to what went before and what came after, like the links of a chain.

If the approach this book takes has a special advantage, it is to be found in storytelling. It is perhaps acceptable to tell some of the stories from the Church's past with no attempt even to summarize the entire story from beginning to end. At the same time, however, when possible I try to point out important connections between the events narrated in this book.

One of the most important lessons a volume such as this one can offer is that change in the Church is not only nothing to fear but is necessary for the Church to remain faithful to its true identity. In the words of Hubert Jedin: "As the grain of wheat germinates and sprouts, produces stalk and ear, yet always remains wheat, so does the Church's nature manifest itself in changing forms during the course of history, but remains always true to itself."

To read a book such as this one is to learn again how human the Church has been and is. For while Christ did not leave the Church entirely to its own resources, he did make it dependent on human choices and human strengths and weaknesses. In addition to its many saints, at its highest levels the Church has had its share of narrow-minded nitwits, not to mention the occasional scoundrel or fool.

At the same time, even during episodes when the Church's leaders and institutions were most corrupt, the inner life of the Spirit continued to inspire and guide many Christian men and women whose stories are lost to historical research. The Church's sacraments nourished the life of the people of God and God's Word in the human words of Scripture, comforted and challenged. In this sense, it is unfortunate that a volume such as this one must largely confine itself to the activities and words of ecclesiastical "movers and shakers."

There are stories in this book of times when the Church was not healthy, at least on those levels most accessible to historians. But recall that the Holy Spirit works for good through the failings of the people of God and its leaders as well as through their virtues.

Hubert Jedin explains that to pretend that the Church is perfect is to forget that its nature is not purely spiritual. Rather, the Church constantly strives to move from the dark into the light:

> The growth of the Church is sometimes hindered through internal or external causes; she suffers sickness, and experiences both reverses and periods of renewed vitality. She does not appear as the Bride without spot or stain, as those who believe

in a purely "spiritual" Church in all ages have fondly thought her to be, but covered with the dust of centuries, suffering through the failures of men and persecuted by her enemies. Church history is therefore the theology of the Cross. Without injury to her essential holiness, the Church is not perfect . . . she is in constant need of renewal. Although she is never to be superseded in the world of space and time by a "spiritual" Church, she retains a provisional character and awaits perfection.

Finally, I wrote this book because I care deeply about the Church and about the Catholic way of life in today's world. My purpose is to inform and encourage, but I try to entertain as well. It implies no disrespect that from time to time, when a particular event allows for it, I try to make room for a smile. I have yet to come across a rule which requires that a book such as this one be sobersided from beginning to end.

For the early Christians, Jesus was not a figure of the past, but rather the risen Lord present and active in their midst. The Gospels, then, present Jesus of Nazareth *in the light of his ultimate identity as the risen Christ.* The most fundamental theme of Jesus' teaching was that a new form of God's gift of salvation — spiritual healing and liberation — was offered to humankind.

Jesus of Nazareth

The Church's one foundation," says the old hymn, "is Jesus Christ her Lord." Without Jesus there would be no Church. Thus, there can be little worthwhile discussion of key events in the Church's history without some understanding of the historical Jesus.

Virtually all that historians can learn about Jesus of Nazareth comes from the New Testament. One of the first things Scripture scholars insist upon today, however, is that it is difficult to locate information in the New Testament that can qualify as "pure" historical data.

This should come as no surprise. After all, the New Testament developed at a time when people had different questions than people have today. First-century Christians were not much interested in what the twentieth century calls history. Neither were they interested in reading a biography of Jesus as that term is used today. Rather, they asked questions about meaning. What did Jesus and his message mean? What difference does he make? How are we to understand our here-and-now experience of the risen Christ?

"If the Gospels were not biographies of Jesus," wrote Scripture scholar Gerard Sloyan, "what were they? They were an attempt from four different viewpoints to help people share in the life of the one whom the early Church believed in as 'the Christ.' The four whose Gospels survive were convinced that Jesus still lived, not just in memory but in fact."[1]

A statement in John's Gospel could easily apply to the other three Gospels, too: "But these [things] are written so that you may come to *believe* that Jesus is the Messiah, the Son of God, and that through believing you *may have life in his name*" (20:31, emphasis added).

The writers of the twenty-seven New Testament documents had no interest in recording the kind of material that the modern world puts in newspapers and books. In the words of Church historian Thomas Bokenkotter, "The Gospels were not meant to be a historical or biographical account of Jesus. . . . Their authors did not deliberately invent or falsify facts about Jesus, but they were not primarily concerned with historical accuracy."[2]

For the early Christians, Jesus was not a figure of the past, but rather the risen Lord present and active in their midst. The Gospels, then, present Jesus of Nazareth *in the light of his ultimate identity as the risen Christ.*

The critical thing to understand—and there will be a more detailed discussion of this in Chapter 3—is that the Gospels developed in stages over a period of forty to sixty years. This process included much prayerful reflection on who Jesus was and upon his meaning for various Christian communities.

Consequently, there has never been a time since the death and resurrection of Jesus that he and his teachings have not been interpreted to meet the needs of specific faith communities. Even the New Testament reveals a variety of perspectives on Jesus and on Christian faith, some of which actually contradict one another. So, when believers today find differing perspectives on Jesus and on what it means to live a Christian life, it can be helpful to recall that this has been going on since the dawn of Christianity. It's nothing new.[3]

One example of different but complementary interpretations of Jesus is the way the Gospels of Matthew and Luke portray him.

Throughout his Gospel, Matthew, writing for a Jewish-Christian audience, presents Jesus as the new Moses. This is how Matthew helped his first readers to make connections between their Jewish roots and their newfound Christian faith.

Luke, on the other hand, wrote for a gentile-Christian audience, so he portrays Jesus in ways that will make sense to people whose culture is Greco-Roman and who know little about the Old Testament or Judaism.

Luke, writing for a comfortable, middle-class audience, is quite harsh with those who are wealthy. His Jesus curses those who are rich and blesses those who are poor (see 6:20–25).

Matthew, however, portrays Jesus in quite a different way. Writing for a poor audience, he has Jesus teach that riches can be a serious threat to one's destiny in this world and in eternity (see 13:22), but he says that with God all things are possible (see 19:26). All people are called to be poor in spirit, and even the wealthy should hunger and thirst after justice (see 5:3–6).

Interpretations of Jesus so heavily influence the Gospels that it is difficult to be sure when words of Jesus or stories about Jesus constitute uninterpreted data from the historical Jesus of Nazareth. The problem is that in order to identify historical material in the Gospels the historian must understand that he or she can reach that level only by "filtering out" other true and inspired but, most likely, nonhistorical material. This, however, is easier said than done. Literary material from the various stages in the development of the Gospels is so closely woven together that scholars find it difficult to distinguish one stage from another.

In reading a Gospel story about or saying of Jesus, the historian must ask: How much of this is based on an unmodified recollection of the historical Jesus? How much surfaced at other stages in the development of the Gospels to answer specific questions at particular times and in particular places and situations?

To identify material in the Gospels that is unquestionably historical is a tricky business. This does not mean that some parts of the Gospels are untrue. On the contrary, the Gospels communicate religious truths from beginning to end. But not every word in the Gospels is historical.

As the Second Vatican Council's document on divine revelation declares, the only material in the Bible that is guaranteed to be without error is the information that is "necessary for our salvation." Whether Jesus had twelve disciples or twelve hundred is irrelevant to our salvation. That Jesus died and was raised from the dead is, however, "necessary for our salvation" (*Dogmatic Constitution on Divine Revelation,* no. 11).

When reading the Gospels it is critical to ask: What is the inspired truth intended here by the writer? In the words of the great French Scripture scholar Xavier Léon-Dufour, S.J., "the reader of the Bible has to look for God's Word in language which both manifests and yet veils it."[4]

One principle accepted by most Catholic Scripture scholars goes like this: Anything in the Gospels that cannot be discovered in the Judaism of Jesus' time or in primitive Christianity most likely came from the historical Jesus of Nazareth.

A given story about or saying of Jesus in the Gospels may have been adapted in order to meet the needs of a specific community. All the same, this story or saying carries the truth of Christ regardless of the extent to which it reflects what an actual observer of the event would have seen and heard.

This is frustrating to the modern historian, who has many questions about the personalities of the persons involved, exactly who said what, when, and who else was there, how they were dressed, what the weather was like that day, who agreed and who disagreed, and what happened next. Yet, that such a process was at work in the development of the Gospels is perfectly understandable and acceptable.

In the first century, just as today, it was necessary to adapt stories about Jesus to unique historical and cultural contexts. Indeed, it was precisely through this process that divineinspiration took place. In other words, the Gospels are primarily documents of faith, not historical records.

Historians are careful, therefore, about what they say is historical in the Gospels and what is true in other ways. Still, there is no doubt that Jesus actually existed and that he was born at a certain point in human history. Even the lyrical Prologue of John's Gospel, which calls Jesus "the Word" and emphasizes his divine nature to a degree that the other Gospels do not, insists upon taking Jesus' historical presence and human nature with absolute seriousness. "In the beginning was the Word, and the Word was with God, and the Word was God" (1:1), John's Gospel declares. Yet a few verses later, we read: "The Word became flesh, he lived among us . . ." (1:14).

At the same time, the Gospels say nothing about Jesus' physical appearance, how tall he was or the color of his hair. Likewise with regard to exactly how he dressed, what kind of personality he had, or anything about his psychology. The Gospels are singularly obscure about Jesus' awareness of himself, and theologians argue to this day about the nature of Jesus' awareness of his divinity.

It is certain that Jesus of Nazareth did not look like the portraits in museums of a light-skinned Jesus, pictures painted over the centuries by European artists. Jesus was a Palestinian Jewish villager and would not look out of place among the people who live in Palestinian villages today. Compared to the average North American, these people are short of stature, and they have dark skin and dark hair. Undoubtedly, this is what Jesus looked like, too.

Of course, Jesus did not resemble modern pious pictures that seem to portray him either as a romanticized captain of the football team, or as blond, blue-eyed, and almost effeminate. Many of the more gruesome portraits of Jesus produced by Catholic piety over the years are equally impossible to reconcile with what Jesus must have looked like.

Every age and every culture produces images of Jesus for a given people at a particular time and place. It is perfectly appropriate for this to be so; however, no one should confuse such images with the historical Jesus about whose physical appearance the Gospels say nothing.

It is a plain fact that a biography of Jesus, in the modern sense, will never be possible. That said, however, scholars also insist that it is possible to sketch an outline of what we know about the historical Jesus. Such experts as Scripture scholars Joseph Fitzmyer, S.J. and Luke Timothy Johnson and Church historian Karl Baus give such summary descriptions.[5]

We know, says Fitzmyer, that Jesus was a Palestinian Jew whose mother's name was Mary, and that she was married to a man named Joseph, who was a carpenter. Jesus was born about the year 4 B.C. (a quirk of the calendar caused by a later historical miscalculation) and lived in a town in Galilee called Nazareth.[6]

Jesus began preaching and teaching in public about A.D. 28, and his ministry was somehow related to that of John the Baptist. At least in the beginning, he centered his activities in a town called Capernaum, in Galilee, but they were not limited to that area. The actual length of Jesus' public ministry is uncertain because of conflicting accounts among the Gospels, but it may have been about three years.

As a Jewish teacher, Jesus was influenced by the ethical and religious teachings of his era. Sometimes he disagreed with other Jewish teachers, and this showed up particularly in disagreements with Pharisees, Sadducees, "and others," says Fitzmyer, "who professed to be interpreters of the Hebrew Scriptures for the people."[7]

Jesus gathered together a group of followers, most notably Simon—whose name Jesus later changed to Peter—and his brother Andrew, and John and James whose father's name was Zebedee. Twelve of these followers

Jesus associated with on a particularly close basis, but it is not possible to tell what the relationship was between the Twelve and other disciples of Jesus. Neither is it possible to know for sure the names of the Twelve because the lists in the Gospels differ. It is also difficult to discover whether Jesus taught a definite way of life to his followers.

Eventually, Jesus' preaching and teaching brought him to Jerusalem where, about the time of the Jewish feast of the Passover, one of the Twelve, Judas Iscariot, betrayed him and Jesus was arrested. The Jewish leaders questioned Jesus and brought him before Pontius Pilate, the Roman official in charge of Judea, who sentenced him to death. Jesus died by crucifixion outside the city walls and was buried the same day.

Some days later, on Sunday, Jesus' tomb was discovered to be empty. Soon, many of his followers reported that they had encountered Jesus alive, that he was "raised" from the dead.

We know that the historical Jesus' ministry was one of preaching and teaching, but exactly what did he say? "Even though modern New Testament interpreters scrutinize every saying or teaching put on Jesus' lips by the evangelists," comments Fitzmyer, "there is a general agreement about certain themes of his authentic teaching. . . ."[8]

The most fundamental theme of Jesus' teaching was that a new form of God's gift of salvation — spiritual healing and liberation — was offered to humankind. Whereas before, salvation was offered almost exclusively to the Jewish people, now in Jesus, says Fitzmyer, "this new and final divine offer of salvation was made to all human beings, to the poor, to the outcasts, to sinners, perhaps even to Samaritans, and non-Jews who would come to him. . . ."[9]

Jesus invited people to "repent and believe" this Good News; to set aside fear and worry in order to believe in God's love; and to reject self-centeredness in order to give loving service to others. Jesus insisted, says Karl Baus, that purity of mind and intention is the basis for moral behavior, "thus giving the individual conscience the decisive role in the sphere of religion."[10]

The second theme of Jesus' teaching stressed the basic validity of what the Hebrew Scriptures, or Old Testament, had taught. But Jesus insisted on the deeper, spiritual meaning of the old tradition. He taught that more important than legalistic religious observances is helping one's neighbor in need.

Jesus shocked many of his contemporaries by saying that sinners and outcasts, tax collectors and prostitutes, would be welcome in his

Father's kingdom. He also called people to follow him with no regard for self.

Finally, Jesus did not preach a perspective compatible with an individualistic religion. Rather, life in community is an unavoidable consequence of taking seriously the teachings of Jesus. It's not possible to be a follower of Jesus in isolation from others.

There is no doubt that Jesus lived the kind of life presented by the Gospels, that he was an itinerant preacher, and that he taught in the ways the Gospels portray him as teaching. Jesus was a captivating teller of stories. Scholars believe that the core of the historical Jesus' teaching went something like this: "The kingdom of God is at hand, so repent!" (see Mark 1:15).

Jesus accepted all people, men and women, rich and poor, fellow Jew or foreigner; but he had a special affection for those who were kicked around or ignored by the rest of society—the poor, women, and those whom society despised for racial or religious reasons.

Jesus was a man of prayer who challenged human and religious traditions and customs when taken as ends in themselves, and he embodied the message of salvation, spiritual healing, and liberation, by curing people who were variously afflicted.

The main thing Jesus insisted upon was acceptance of God's will in all things. His central commandment was to love God with one's whole self and other people as oneself. Even enemies must be loved.

For Jesus, love of God and other people was the purpose of life; everything else was mere popcorn. Indeed, so closely united are love of God and love of neighbor for Jesus that while neither may be neglected, to do one is also to do the other.

For the Jesus who walked the dusty roads of Palestine, who shared meals and went to feasts and celebrations with his friends, who kept company with "unacceptable" people, to be open to the kingdom of God was to embrace a set of values and attitudes that would put one at odds with the perspectives of "the world." In modern language, "the world" is "the dominant culture," "the establishment," or "the status quo."

At no time in history has it been acceptable for a Christian to take his or her baptism seriously and not be countercultural. The Christian is wary of what "everyone else is doing" and takes a wait-and-see stance with regard to values and attitudes most people accept without question. At the same time, the Christian celebrates the true and the good wherever they may be found.

Nothing is more certain about the historical Jesus than this: On the night before he was tortured and executed by the Roman authorities as a political criminal, Jesus instructed his disciples to continue what later came to be called the Lord's Supper, the Eucharist or, in the Middle Ages, the Mass. The earliest account of this appears not in one of the Gospels but in Paul's First Letter to the Corinthians:

> For I received from the Lord and also handed on to you, that the Lord Jesus on the night when he was betrayed took a loaf of bread, and when he had given thanks, he broke it and said, "This is my body that is for you. Do this in remembrance of me." In the same way he took the cup also, after supper, saying, "This cup is the new covenant in my blood. Do this, as often as you drink it, in remembrance of me" (11:23–25).

The Gospels of Matthew, Mark, Luke, and John all agree that something mysterious and astounding, something beyond space and time, yet in space and time, happened to Jesus after his burial. The Gospels call this event "resurrection"—a word that expresses in a real and true but limited fashion what happened to Jesus. "Resurrection" is theological shorthand for an event neither the human intellect nor human language can fully understand.

There is no telling what a modern scientist would experience could he or she travel back in time to observe the actual event of Jesus' resurrection. Certainly today there is no historical evidence available. What we have are the Gospel stories of encounters with the risen Christ; there are no descriptions of the Resurrection itself.

What is beyond doubt are the transforming effects of the Resurrection on the lives of countless believers over nearly two thousand years of history. "Regardless of what anyone may personally think or believe about him," wrote historian Jaroslav Pelikan, "Jesus of Nazareth has been the dominant figure in the history of Western culture for almost twenty centuries."[11]

For the Church historian, then, the bottom line is this: It is an irrefutable historical fact that the life, teachings, death, and resurrection of Jesus of Nazareth constitute "the Church's one foundation." Every subsequent event in the Catholic Church's nearly twenty centuries of existence resulted from what theologians call "the Christ event," and there is no adequate understanding of the Church today apart from an experience of that event here and now.

Antioch, in central Asia Minor, appears to have been the first major site outside Palestine where the Gospel was preached, and it was from here that the Church began to spread among non-Jewish peoples.

CHAPTER 2

The Early Church

Christianity began in complete obscurity. It claimed as its founder a Jewish nobody who had been executed as a common troublemaker. It was promoted by yokels whose ideas educated people laughed at. Most of those attracted to Christianity in its earliest years were people with no social status, especially the poor, slaves, and women. Christian bashing was popular for more than two centuries. All the same, within four hundred years Christianity became the dominant religion in the vast and powerful Roman Empire.

The first two hundred and fifty years of Christianity's existence, often in the midst of persecution, constituted an era in Church history that saw the development of the theological ideas and institutions upon which all subsequent

Church history would build. It was these unrepeatable foundational events that gave the Church its lasting shape and character.

Following his death and burial, the disciples of Jesus encountered him as mysteriously but recognizably present among them. It was this experience of the risen Christ that brought the disciples together and made them a community. This much is clear from the early sections of the Acts of the Apostles.

At the same time, however, it is important to understand that the Acts of the Apostles is history primarily in a theological, not a journalistic or textbook sense. To begin with, the early Church in Acts is idealized. It is therefore important to take the humanity of the first Christians seriously enough to presume that there was more tension and human conflict during the Church's earliest years than the Acts of the Apostles reveals.

In writing Acts, it's as if the author was saying to the reader, "Pay attention; here is the ideal we must strive for, here is the perfect community of faith."

That does not mean, of course, that there is no reliable history in the Acts of the Apostles. The Church traces its birth to a powerful religious experience shared by the assembled disciples and Mary, the mother of Jesus, on the Jewish feast of Pentecost. The language the Acts of the Apostles uses to describe this event—whether intended to communicate inspired truth literally or metaphorically is debatable—conveys how deep and profound the experience was:

> When the day of Pentecost had come, they were all together in one place. And suddenly from heaven there came a sound like the rush of a violent wind, and it filled the entire house where they were sitting. Divided tongues, as of fire, appeared among them, and a tongue rested on each of them (Acts 2:1–3).

The faith of the first followers of Christ was based on their personal experience of an event of great power, an experience of healing, freedom, and peace. They were "filled with the Holy Spirit"—a phrase which expresses but feebly an experience that transcends human words—and became confident witnesses of the risen Christ. The reader learns that they "were faithful to the teaching of the apostles," and shared a loving community that included prayer together and the "breaking of the bread"— New Testament language for the Eucharist (see Acts 2:42–47).

Note that these early gatherings of the community of faith took place in people's homes

(Acts 2:46). This is perfectly consistent with the Jewish roots of the first Christians, for even today in the Jewish community the home, not the synagogue, is the center of religious life.

One of the great blessings of modern times is a rediscovery of this tradition in Catholicism. "The family," said Pope John Paul II in 1978, "is the basic unit of society and of the Church."[1] The family in its various forms, including childless married couples, single-parent families, and "blended" families, not the parish, is the basic cell of the Church.

The leaders of the first Christian community, in Jerusalem, were twelve men whom, the Gospels tell us, Jesus himself chose. While the existence of this group is difficult to confirm historically—the Gospels give different lists of names for the Twelve, for example—its theological purpose is clear. In Israel there were twelve tribes; so the Twelve symbolize the New Israel, the Church.

Later a man named Stephen, one of seven designated as deacons, became the first Christian martyr. Stephen was a Jewish convert who incurred the wrath of the Temple leaders in Jerusalem by proclaiming that the Scriptures had been fulfilled in Jesus of Nazareth. The Jewish leaders became enraged at this and ordered Stephen stoned to death (see Acts 6:8–7:60).

The Acts of the Apostles says that the leader of the Jerusalem community was Peter. Paul, whose letters are older by about twenty years than Mark, the earliest Gospel, says that Peter was the first to see the risen Jesus. The Acts of the Apostles portrays Peter as the first to proclaim the Gospel and the first to work a miracle. This and other New Testament evidence makes it clear that Peter had a priority of leadership among the first Christians.

Other important figures in the Jerusalem community were James, who evidently succeeded Peter when he later left to become a missionary, and John, whom Acts associates closely with Peter. When modern Christians struggle with issues related to leadership in the Church, therefore, it is important to remember that institutionalized leadership structures are rooted in the Church's earliest days.

Scholars know little about the early Christian community in Jerusalem. Evidently, however, these early Christians did not at first think of themselves as separate from Judaism. "For a time," explained Thomas Bokenkotter, "the Church remained completely Jewish, a sect within Israel of those who believed in the resurrection of Jesus and regarded him as the promised Messiah who was about to come again to definitely establish the reign of God."[2]

The Acts of the Apostles notes that the disciples gathered each day in the Temple for prayer (2:46). Some Jewish leaders wanted to expel the followers of Jesus from their midst, but popular opinion was in their favor. Many Jews admired the little group for their faith and love for Jewish tradition. This is one source of today's renewed appreciation for the Church's Jewish roots and heritage.

It appears that followers of Christ first carried the message of the Gospel only to their fellow Jews. It was only gradually that theChristian community moved away from Jerusalem, and the cause for this departure apparently was the increased tension between Rome and the Jewish people in Jerusalem. Between the years 66 and 70, the Jewish people revolted against Roman domination, and it was then, before the destruction of the Temple and final Roman victory, that the Jewish Christians in Jerusalem seem to have migrated to Pella in northern Greece.

It is likely that the first to approach the gentiles with the Gospel were Jewish Christians who differed with the leaders in Jerusalem on the role of the Temple in worship. Stephen was a leader of this group, and his martyrdom kicked off the first full-scale persecution of the disciples of Jesus. When Stephen's followers dispersed to other parts of the Roman Empire they carried the Gospel with them.

Antioch, in central Asia Minor, appears to have been the first major site outside Palestine where the Gospel was preached, and it was from here that the Church began to spread among non-Jewish peoples. It was this development, too, that led to the first doctrinal controversy, one which is clear from the Acts of the Apostles and the letters of Saint Paul.

Was it necessary for gentile converts to Christianity to also become observant Jews? Did converts need to fulfill the letter of the Jewish Law before they could be baptized? The more traditional among the first Christians said yes, gentile converts needed also to become good Jews in order to be baptized. The "progressives" said no, there was no such need.

The most important figure in settling this dispute was a man named Paul. A convert to Christianity and a former gung-ho persecutor of Christians, Paul insisted that Christian faith did not require Jewish observance. It was Paul who shaped the Gospel to appeal to all humankind.

Paul believed with all his heart that only faith in the risen Christ was necessary. In fact, he taught that Christian faith brought liberation from the Mosaic Law, a move perfectly in tune with Jesus' opposition to religious legalism.

As nearly as the event can be reconstructed, it seems that a ferocious conflict developed over this issue, especially in Antioch, where a large part of the Christian population was gentile. Jewish Christians in Antioch, who had previously been laid-back about joining in the common meals in the context of which the Eucharist was celebrated, began to waffle. Even Peter decided to comply in order to get along with the "Judaizers."

Then Paul arrived and raised the roof. He insisted that it was a betrayal of the Gospel to force gentiles to observe the Jewish Law in order to be baptized. Paul even gave Peter, in public, a large and long-winded piece of his mind. It was not without precedent, then, when in later centuries saints, theologians, and other personages felt free to call various popes to task for behavior or decisions that seemed contrary to the spirit of the Gospel. For Paul, the underlying principle was that even Church leaders always must take the Gospel as their ultimate standard.

About the year 49, what is sometimes called the Council of Jerusalem took place, and Church historians often refer to this as the first Church council. After many long and conflict-filled debates, Peter stood up to support Paul's position. Gentile converts, he said, should not be required to observe the Jewish Law. All that was necessary for baptism was faith in the risen Jesus, that is, a personal belief in and relationship with Christ and with the *ekklesia*, the Church or assembly of the faithful.

Christians hear nothing today about avoiding food sacrificed to idols, of course, and this says something about even the decisions of a Church council. Societies and cultures evolve, and Church legislation adapts appropriately. On the other hand, in our time the divorce rate among couples who "live together" before marriage is twice that of couples who do not "live together." So the wisdom of the ancient prohibition against premarital sexual intercourse seems as valid today as it ever was.[3]

In any era, of course, there seem to be some hardline conservatives who refuse to compromise even on issues of secondary importance, and such was the case in this situation. Rightwing "Judaizers" later caused Paul much grief. They visited communities Paul had founded and insisted on a full observance of the Jewish law. The long-term outcome was settled, however: Christianity was now a religion for anyone, regardless of ethnic or religious background.

Paul became the apostle to the gentiles, carrying the Gospel far and wide. His letters in the New Testament reveal him as the first and greatest among the molders of the Church. Paul made three missionary journeys between the years 46 and 58 and founded

Christian communities in what are now Syria, Turkey, Yugoslavia, Greece, and Cyprus. Other Christian communities appeared, too, but their origins are impossible to determine with historical accuracy.

About the middle of the first century, Paul returned to Jerusalem to meet with the leaders of the Church there, for he acknowledged Jerusalem as the first among the local Christian communities. Someone recognized Paul as the former Jewish persecutor of Christians, however, and reported him to the Jewish authorities as a traitor. Paul's life was threatened, and he landed in the slammer for two years in Caesarea. Paul appealed as a Roman citizen to the emperor, who had him brought to Rome, and there he was held under house arrest for another two years.

According to scholarly consensus, the Roman authorities viewed Paul as a leader of a Jewish sect that could undermine the authority of the government, and he was executed about the year 64.

Peter's fate is even more obscure. After the so-called Council of Jerusalem and a visit to Antioch in about A.D. 50, little is known about him after he left Jerusalem to become a missionary. Tradition places Peter in Rome at the time of his death by execution in the mid-60s. Excavations beneath Saint Peter's

Basilica in Rome in recent decades turned up remarkable evidence, however, that the great church's main altar does, in fact, rest high above but directly over the final burial place of Peter.[4]

By the close of the first century, Christianity was attracting converts from the upper classes of Roman society. Scholars know that a Roman official by the name of Blabrio was executed in part for being a Christian. There also is a fascinating description by Pliny the Younger, a Roman governor, of Christian behavior in first-century Rome:

> [Christians said] that it was their habit on a fixed day to assemble before daylight and recite by turns a form of words to Christ as a god; and that they bound themselves with an oath, not for any crime, but not to commit theft or robbery or adultery, not to break their word, and not to deny a deposit when demanded. After this was done their custom was to depart, and to meet again to take food, but ordinary and harmless food. . . .[5]

From the late first century into the second there were sporadic persecutions of Christians. During this time also, Christians began to develop new prayers in addition to those they inherited from Judaism, and these new prayers were characterized by a deep sense of hope and thanksgiving.

As noted above, institutional developments began to take place almost immediately when Matthias took the place of Judas and with the appointing of the seven deacons. These developments continued through the early centuries of the Church. Deacons continued to hold a place of special importance, but soon another form of leadership emerged in men called "presbyters" or "overseers." Originally, these two titles referred to the same office, but eventually they became two different functions.

"Overseers" and "presbyters" developed into what the modern Church calls bishops and priests. The deaths of the apostles by the end of the first century made it especially critical to establish institutional forms of leadership. Saint Ignatius of Antioch, who died about A.D. 110, developed in his letters a theology to support the idea of a "monarchical" approach to the office of bishop. According to Ignatius, the bishop has ultimate authority, and this perspective on leadership became the universal one throughout the Church by the middle of the third century. Without the popularity of Ignatius' "monarchical" view of the bishop's role, the bishop of Rome might never have gained his primary place in the Church.

During these first two centuries, one of the greatest challenges to Christianity came in the form of various teachings that were incompatible with the new faith. A writer named Celsus, about the year 180, wrote a document called *True Discourse*, which accused Christ of having attracted followers through lies and witchcraft.

The early Christian writers who responded to such charges by explaining their faith were called *apologists*, from Latin and Greek words which mean "to defend and justify." Perhaps the most famous of the early apologists was Saint Justin Martyr (c. 100–165). Justin became a Christian in 130 and defended Christianity in writings addressed to the Roman emperor Antoninus Pius, to the Roman senate, and in a document addressed to "Trypho the Jew."

Justin insisted that Jesus was the Messiah, that he fulfilled Old Testament messianic prophecies, and that his death and resurrection were the means of salvation for all who believe in him. He also wrote that the rite of baptism was the means of entrance into new life in Christ, and that the Eucharist was the means to sustain such a life. Justin called Christianity "the only certain and adequate philosophy," and inisisted that if given a chance Christians would show themselves responsible citizens.

For all the value of their writings to later centuries, the apologists did not prevent the attacks of the Roman emperors for long. During the reign of the philosopher-emperor Marcus Aurelius, who followed Antoninus Pius, persecutions began again, and Justin was executed.

During these early decades of the Church's history, one of the most tenacious threats to authentic Christian faith emerged within the Church itself. Called Gnosticism, this heresey has resurfaced, in one form or another, over and over again down through the centuries. Gnosticism was a system of philosophical thought which taught that salvation is available only through a knowledge (Greek, *gnosis*) that answers the basic human questions about the meaning of life and the world.

Gnosticism was dualistic, that is, it taught that matter is evil, only the spirit is good. The world was created not by God but by a lesser deity called the *Demiurge*. The human soul is trapped in the physical body, but some people have a divine spark within them that can help them return to God. This is an elite group called the *Spirituals*, who are separate from the rest of humankind, which has no hope for salvation. Christ's purpose, said the Gnostics, was to bring this special knowledge to those destined to return to God. Of course, Christ could not possibly have been human, because the flesh is evil. Gnosticism taught that Jesus only appeared to be human.

This notion that the body is bad, that the soul must be rescued from the body, has plagued Christianity even down to our own time. It has led countless people to mistrust human sexuality to the point, for example, that sexual sins were viewed as the worst form of sin, a perspective alien to Jesus and to the New Testament as a whole.

Another widely influential heretic of the early Christian decades was Marcion (c. 110–60). Marcion taught that the God of the Old Testament and the God of Jesus were totally foreign to each other. Like the Gnostics, Marcion denied the goodness of creation and the possibility that Jesus could really have been human. He rejected marriage because, having such a bodily/sexual dimension, it could not possibly be good.

About the year 170, Montanus was the forerunner of countless fundamentalist Christian sects. He taught that Jesus would return very soon, even to the point of giving details about time and place. Today, as in the second century, announcements that Jesus' return is imminent, no matter how sincere, are best ignored.

Quintus Septimus Florens Tertullian, born about 160, came from a pagan family and was baptized a Christian toward the end of the second century. Some of his Christian writings survive to this day, however, and are valuable for insights into primitive Christian thought. Early in the third century, however, Tertullian left orthodox Christianity and became a Montanist, attracted by this group's rigorous spirituality and their claim that they were guided directly by the Holy Spirit. Tertullian, however, rejected the role of authority claimed by Montanus as well as his claim that Jesus would return soon. In a sense, Tertullian formed a new version of Montanism. Upon his death in 225, however, his system of thought quickly disappeared.

Christianity was incompatible with the Montanism of both Montanus and Tertullian. Even this early in the Church's history, authentic Christian faith exhibited a powerful tendency to seek balance. The Church refused to encourage extremes in spirituality or to support those who decided that they were better than everyone else, "the only true Christians."

The Church also rejected any perspective that claimed to depend directly on the Holy Spirit for its authority. Instead, the Church insisted on the objective guidance of the bishops as the successors of the apostles. Also, by rejecting the "easy out" of belief in a Second Coming that was just around the corner, the Church proclaimed that Christians are to face the future with practical realism, courage, and hope.

By the end of the second century, the Church was strong but still officially disapproved by the Roman government. Then, in the year 202 Roman authorities published an edict forbidding conversion to Christianity, and the next year a group of catechumens — those preparing for baptism — were arrested and executed.

Emperors came and went, some sympathetic or indifferent to Christianity, others of a mind to persecute Christians. In A.D. 244–49, an emperor ruled named Philip the Arab, and he was well-disposed toward the Christians. Unfortunately, his successor, Decius, was the worst news yet for the followers of Christ. During the two years he reigned, Decius insisted that the old Roman religion be revived and that everyone must offer sacrifice to the gods or be killed. During this time Fabian, bishop of Rome, was executed, and many Christians betrayed their faith.

Decius's successor, Gallerius (260–68), launched persecutions in order to bring money into the government's treasury. He confiscated Church property and imposed fines for being a Christian.

Lest anyone think it absurd for a government to kill people simply for being Christians, something the enlightened twentieth century would never tolerate, consider not only the many priests and nuns who died in the Nazi death camps of World War II but also Central

America during the 1970s and 1980s, where cruel military governments murdered many people for nothing more than giving religious instructions or feeding and clothing the poor. These are but two examples of the persecution of Christians in what has been called the bloodiest of all centuries.

Persecutions alternated with periods of relative peace for the Church. In the midst of such uncertainty, however, Christianity continued to make headway. The first theological schools appeared in Antioch and Alexandria, giving rise to various ways of interpreting Scriptutre. One approach insisted on an allegorical view of Scripture; another said Scripture must be interpreted literally. The more things change, goes the saying, the more they stay the same. One of the hottest questions among Christians of various stripes today is how to read and interpret the Bible.

Theological developments continued as well. The Church decided that baptism should require a lengthy period of preparation, called the *catechumenate,* because it was considered important that those who asked for baptism should understand the differences between the Christian and pagan ways of life before being baptized. Today, again, there is a renewed emphasis on understanding that the Christian life in any era is likely to clash in some ways with the status quo and the dominant culture. This can't help but happen among a people who pledge to base their lives on love of God and neighbor above all else.

The Eucharist, too, went through a process of development. By the year 220, the Eucharist had evolved from two separate services, the service of the Word and the Fellowship Meal, to one unified service. One of the most important insights of the Second Vatican Council (1962–65) was the need to give both parts of the Mass—the liturgy of the Word and the liturgy of the Eucharist—their proper prominence.

Penance and reconciliation required attention also, especially in the context of a need to deal with people who weakened in the face of persecution and later asked to return to the community. Some argued for a very strict position, others argued for leniency. In the end, the position based on compassion and forgiveness won out, much to the early Church's credit.

Institutional developments also continued. The bishop became the symbol of unity, the main leader of the community, and the primary presider at the Eucharist. Other clerical offices emerged, too, however. Deacons were called the "ear, mouth, heart, and soul" of the bishop. Presbyters, or priests, gradually were delegated to care for smaller communities and to preside at the Eucharist in the bishop's absence. By the mid–third century, according to a list from Rome, there were "forty-six presbyters, seven deacons, seven subdeacons, forty-two acolytes, fifty-two exorcists, readers, and doorkeepers." Today's renewed appreciation for the variety of ministries in the Church is rooted in those early developments.

In the year 300 came the last terrible Roman persecution, under the emperor Diocletian. By this time, Christians constituted about 20 percent of the population in the empire, but Diocletian was determined to eradicate Christianity. In 303, he ordered the destruction of all Christian places of worship, that all Christian writings be turned over to the government, and that all clergy be arrested. True to established form for persecutions, he also insisted that everyone must offer sacrifice to the old gods.

During this time, many Christians died for refusing to deny their faith, although the persecution ebbed and flowed from time to time and place to place in the empire. Finally, in 311, after the death of Diocletian, the new emperor, another Gallerius, issued an edict of toleration that gave Christians the freedom to practice their religion.

Gailerius's sympathetic attitude was but a hint of changes to come; changes that would have both light and dark sides for the future of the Church.

Although it is true to say that in general a consensus existed on the present twenty-seven New Testament books by the end of the fourth century, it was only some twelve centuries later, at the fourth session of the Council of Trent in 1546, that the Church defined officially what constitutes the New Testament. These twenty-seven documents, no more and no less, said the council, make up the inspired body, or "canon," of Christian writings.

CHAPTER 3

The Church Gives Birth to the New Testament

The early Christian communities came into existence prior to and without the aid of any specifically Christian sacred writings. Indeed, the only Scriptures the early Christians had were those they received from Judaism. The Hebrew Scriptures, or Old Testament documents, that exist today were collected and approved by the rabbis only about the end of the first century. In the mid-50s, when Saint Paul referred to "scripture" in his letters, what he meant was various parts of the Jewish sacred writings that Christians later called the Old Testament. The same is true of the many similar references in the Gospels.

Paul began his Letter to the Romans, for example, with these words: "From Paul, a servant of Christ Jesus, called to be an apostle, set apart for the service of the gospel that God promised long ago through his prophets in *the holy scriptures*" (1:1–2, emphasis added).

In Matthew's Gospel, Jesus says: "But all this has taken place, so that the *scriptures* of the prophets may be fulfilled" (26:56, emphasis added).

The Church preceded the New Testament writings and, through a process that lasted about seventy years — from the death and resurrection of Jesus, about the year 30, until the end of the first century — gave birth to the various documents that eventually constituted the New Testament. This fact is important to understanding the origins of the New Testament, but it is also essential to reading and interpreting the New Testament today. This is so because only if the reader takes seriously the historical character of the New Testament writings can he or she understand the scriptural Word of God here and now.

First came the life, teachings, death, and resurrection of Jesus. (Remember that "resurrection" is a word the Gospels use to describe a real but mysterious event beyond the grasp of the human mind.) Then came the profound Pentecost happenings, which signaled the birth of the Church. Following these foundational Christian events, of greatest significance to the first Christians was the experience of the risen Christ in their midst, in their dedication to service and communal prayer, for this experience brought salvation. (Remember too that "salvation" may best be described as an ongoing, lifelong process of spiritual healing, liberation, and peace; a process that begins in this life but comes to completion only in the next life.)

When the earliest Christians assembled to share a fellowship meal, as a part of this gathering they read from the Jewish sacred writings, which they interpreted in the light of the life, teachings, death, and resurrection of Jesus, and they shared the bread and the cup as Jesus had instructed the disciples on the night before he died. It was in such settings as this that the Gospels began to take shape.

In 1964 the Pontifical Biblical Commission published a document entitled *Concerning the Historical Truth of the Gospels*. This official Church document explains that there are "three stages of tradition by which the doctrine and the life of Jesus have come down to us."[1] These stages may be designated as the stage of the historical Jesus, the storytelling, or oral tradition stage, and the stage of the written text.

In other words, first came Jesus of Nazareth, then came the stories told and retold countless times about Jesus in the years following his death and resurrection, and finally came the Gospels of Matthew, Mark, Luke, and John in their original Greek manuscripts.

The first stage, that of the historical Jesus, has already been discussed in Chapter 1. The important thing to keep in mind is that only insofar as one can "pass through" the subsequent oral and written stages as they are evident in the Gospels is it possible to identify the historical Jesus. Even then, the issue of historicity in the Gospels is enormously complex.[2]

Stage two, which took place between the death and resurrection of Jesus and the writing of Mark, the first Gospel, was the time during which the earliest Christian communities interpreted the memories of those who had seen, heard, and touched Jesus in the light of his death and resurrection. These stories were also told and retold countless times in answer to the specific needs of particular communities.

A community of gentile, or non-Jewish converts to Christianity, for example, would find it puzzling to try to make sense of the

Jewish religion and culture that constituted the world in which Jesus lived. Therefore, those who told the stories of Jesus to gentile communities had to interpret Jesus and his teachings in ways that would make sense to gentiles. This interpretation process included the need to explain certain Jewish traditions and institutions, as well as key Aramaic words, since that is the language Jesus spoke.

Jewish converts to Christianity, on the other hand, needed to have the new faith explained to them in ways that would help them to understand how Jesus was the fulfillment of their Jewish traditions. Those who told stories of Jesus to Jewish communities went to some lengths to show their listeners how Jesus fulfilled Israel's centuries-old longing for the Messiah. They would quote extensively from the prophets and then showed how Jesus had fulfilled their prophecies.

This storytelling or oral tradition stage lasted about forty years, from the death and resurrection of Jesus around the year 30 until the writing of the first Gospel, Mark, which scholarly consensus dates at about 70. Clearly, much storytelling can happen in forty years, and much interpretation was undoubtedly needed in order to make the stories of Jesus meaningful for the various Jewish and gentile Christian communities.

From the earliest days of the Christian faith, believers found it necessary to interpret Jesus' meaning for different audiences. This process has been a part of Christian life down to our own day, when Christians try to interpret Jesus and his message according to the needs of specific times, places, and cultures.

The third stage in the development of the Gospels was the actual writing of Matthew, Mark, Luke, and John. One reason this stage occurred was that the eyewitnesses of Jesus began to die and the Christian communities wanted to preserve the stories of Jesus. At the same time, Christianity had become rooted in the Hellenistic culture of the Roman Empire, which was a culture of the written word.

Scripture scholars call this process of writing the Gospels *redaction,* which means editing, interpreting, and writing. Those who actually wrote the four Gospels are called *redactors.* This term is important because it encapsulates the awareness that the authors of the Gospels were not simply journalists or scribes who wrote down what someone else dictated to them. Rather, they were creatively involved in molding and shaping the materials at their disposal so as to present the gospel in terms best suited to the people they wrote for.

During this redaction stage the authors of the Gospels gathered together stories or oral traditions about Jesus, as well as previously written materials, and shaped what would become known as the Gospels.

Most Catholic and Protestant scripture scholars today believe that the Gospel of Mark was written first, about the year 70, that Matthew and Luke were written about 85, and that John was written between 90 and 100. Of special interest to scholars for many centuries was the fact that Matthew, Mark, and Luke are so similar. Yet they also have significant differences. How to explain this?

Because Matthew and Luke have material in common that is also in Mark, scholarly consensus holds that Matthew and Luke both depended on Mark. However, because Matthew and Luke also have material in common that is not in Mark, it seems that they also both relied on another written source that no longer exists. Scholars call this hypothetical document "Q," from the German word *Quelle*, or "source."

One thing this suggests, explains Scripture scholars John H. Hayes and Carl R. Holladay, is that "one can examine a story or saying of Jesus in Mark, let us say, then examine the same story in either Matthew or Luke, and on the basis of these investigations pinpoint the precise ways in which they have redacted [adapted and interpreted] Mark's version of the story."[3]

Each Gospel was written for a particular Christian audience, and each presents a unique portrait of Jesus and of the Good News of salvation. Mark's Gospel was written for a persecuted and suffering community; therefore Mark portrays Jesus in a way that will be most meaningful to his readers, with an emphasis on his role as the "Son of man" who is persecuted and suffering for the sake of others. "Then he began to teach them," says Mark, "that the Son of man must undergo great suffering, and be rejected by the elders, the chief priests, and the scribes, and killed . . ." (8:31).

Matthew addressed a poor Jewish Christian audience, so the author portrayed Jesus as the new Moses, with many references to how Jesus fulfilled Jewish scriptural prophecies. Moses went up on a mountain and brought back the Ten Commandments. Jesus delivers a Sermon on the Mount in which he gives the new Law of the Beatitudes written in a way to emphasize that material poverty has value only if it nourishes and is a sign of spiritual poverty, that is, complete dependence on God: "How blessed are the poor in spirit . . . Blessed are those who mourn . . . Blessed are the meek . . . Blessed are the merciful . . ." (see 5:1–10).

The Gospel of Luke, on the other hand, addresses issues important to an affluent gentile-Christian community. Therefore, Luke's Jesus delivers his sermon "on a level place" (6:17) and slants it so that those well-off will understand that financial security and material comfort are not without their risks: "Then he looked up at his disciples and said: 'Blessed are you who are poor . . . Blessed are you who are hungry. . . . But woe to you who are rich, for you have received your consolation. Woe, to you who are full now, for you will be hungry'" (see 6:20–26).

Finally, the Gospel of John, which is significantly different in style and content from the first three Gospels, presents Jesus as a divine man. John's Gospel takes seriously Jesus' humanity, but it also places a great deal of emphasis on his divinity: "In the beginning was the Word, and the Word was with God and the Word was God. He was in the beginning with God. All things came into being through him . . ." (1:1–3).

In long discourses, which John placed on the lips of Jesus, it is clear that throughout his Gospel John's Jesus speaks and acts as if the Resurrection is an accomplished fact: "You are from below, I am from above; you are of this world, I am not of this world" (8:23).

Each Gospel, then, is unique both in its style and in its portrayal of Jesus. The Gospels were not, however, the first New Testament documents written. The oral tradition's stories of Jesus were quite enough for a good forty years. The first Christian writings were not Gospels but letters. The oldest documents in the New Testament are the letters of Saint Paul, and the oldest of these is Paul's First Letter to the Thessalonians, written about the year 50.

This is important because it illustrates once again that the first thing the early Christians thought of was not to commission someone to write a Gospel or, much less, a biography of Jesus. Rather, the first priority was to respond in everyday ways to the Gospel message and to the presence of the risen Christ.

This is what Paul's letters reflect, the ongoing efforts of various early Christian communities to be faithful to the Good News of God's love and to respond to the practical and theological issues raised by this new way of life.

At the same time, later Christian authors (perhaps disciples of Paul) wrote letters to Paul. This was a common practice in the ancient world, and no dishonesty attaches to it at all. Many Scripture scholars believe that Paul did not write the Letter to the Ephesians and 1 and 2 Timothy, among others. All the same, the Church accepted these letters by anonymous authors as inspired and included them in the New Testament. The same is true of the Letter to the Hebrews and the First and Second Letters of Peter, which scholars seriously doubt were written by Saint Peter himself.

Others, too, wrote letters and sermons that landed in the New Testament. They all have this in common: The early Church concluded that they faithfully reflected and proclaimed the authentic Gospel message. At the same time, however, the twenty-seven documents that constitute the New Testament sometimes disagree.

For example, Paul says that "Christ is the end of the Law" (Romans 10:4), while in the Gospel of Matthew Jesus says that "until heaven and earth pass away, not one letter, not one stroke of a letter, will pass from the law . . ." (5:18).

Even though these two perspectives seem to contradict each other, in fact both are compatible with Christian faith. Commenting on this, Father Raymond Brown, perhaps the preeminent American Catholic Scripture scholar, says that "these two attitudes have been possible among intelligent Christians ever since: some can stress freedom from the law, some can stress law sanely interpreted, without either group approving libertines or legalists."[4]

The various New Testament documents emerged through human and historical processes, but through these very processes God was at work to communicate the divine word in human words. It also is important to understand, however, that once these documents were written they were not immediately gathered together to form what we call the New Testament. On the contrary, many Gospels were written (see Luke 1:1), but not all of them became Scripture. Many letters and sermons appeared that did not pass muster. It took the Church a long time to compile the New Testament.

How did the Church determine which writings to accept as Scripture and which to reject? Scholars suggest that four criteria were at work.[5]

First, in order to be accepted as Scripture, a document had to have originated, or be reputed to have originated, with an apostle. The Letter to the Hebrews and the Book of Revelation were hotly debated for many years—accepted by some parts of the Church, rejected by others—because there was doubt that they were written by the apostles Paul and John, respectively. With time the understanding of this "apostolic connection" broadened; it was acceptable if a document had been attributed to an apostle. Today, there are serious doubts that any of the New Testament documents have any direct connection with any of Jesus' twelve apostles. Ultimately, what is important is not a direct historical connection with an apostle; rather, what matters is that a given document convey apostolic teaching.

Second, the particular history of specific Christian communities contributed to the survival and ultimate acceptance of the documents that eventually gained acceptance. If these communities had not preserved these writings they would not have survived to be considered by the whole Church.

Third, in order to be accepted as inspired by God, a document had to measure up to the commonly accepted understanding of the meaning of Christian faith.

If a document included material that was clearly contrary to the traditions of the Church, the Church gave it a thumbs-down. The Book of Revelation had an "iffy" status for many decades because of uncertainty about the orthodoxy of its teachings on the second coming of Christ. The Church rejected several Gospels that still exist, including the Gospel of Peter and the Infancy Gospel of Thomas, because they presented teachings at odds with the faith experience of the Church and established Christian doctrines.

The Infancy Gospel of Thomas, for example, written anonymously around the middle of the second century, tells charming legends about the childhood of Jesus. In one story Jesus makes clay sparrows on the Sabbath, and when he claps his hands they fly away. A child who hits Jesus on the shoulder dies immediately. Joseph, the carpenter foster-father of Jesus, cuts a board too short, so Jesus stretches it to the desired length. This Gospel with its

fantastic legends was so popular it was translated into several languages. Troubadors during
the Middle Ages based songs on some of its stories. But the Church did not accept it as a part
of the New Testament because it distorted and
trivialized the Church's beliefs about the humanity and divinity of Jesus.

Fourth, it implies no dishonor to suggest
that chance had something to do with which
writings were included in the New Testament,
especially with regard to such minor documents as the Letter to Philemon and the Letter
of Jude. Chance probably played a part in the
fact that some correspondence from Saint Paul
to the Corinthians was lost. The Holy Spirit
can be at work through happenstance, too.

Not only did it take many years for the
New Testament to come together, but there is
evidence that at various times and places some
Christian communities accepted writings that
the Church ultimately rejected. Part of an
ancient Christian document, called the Muratorian Fragment, which seems to come from
Rome about the year 200, lists two Books of
Revelation, one written by John, one by Peter.
This fragment says, however, that some did not
want the second document read in church. All
the same, the Revelation of Peter was still read
in the Good Friday liturgy in Palestine in the
fifth century.

Not that the Book of Revelation, which made it into the New Testament, had an easy time of it. Rather, it seems to have barely squeaked by. For a long time, many people argued that the Book of Revelation should get the heave-ho because crackpots would interpret it in weird ways. Subsequent history verifies that such concerns were not unfounded, for down to our own time countless characters whose elevator did not go all the way to the top have interpreted the Book of Revelation in ways that give the most spectacular science fiction and fantasy novels a run for their money, and do little, if anything, to nourish a healthy, balanced Christian faith.

By about the year 200, the following were generally approved as Scripture throughout the Church: the Gospels of Matthew, Mark, Luke, and John, the Letters accepted as written by Paul, the Acts of the Apostles, and the First Letters of Peter and John. It took another century before the specific collection of twenty-seven books now in the New Testament were agreed upon. Lists of the documents now in the New Testament date only from the late fourth century. Even then, however, disagreements continued, especially among some of the Eastern churches.

Although it is true to say that in general a consensus existed on the present twenty-seven

New Testament books by the end of the fourth century, it was only some twelve centuries later, at the fourth session of the Council of Trent in 1546, that the Church defined officially what constitute the New Testament. These twenty-seven documents, no more and no less, said the council, make up the inspired body, or "canon," of Christian writings. Why? Because these are the writings that "have come down to us," the writings that have been "preserved in continuous succession" by the Church.[6]

Finally, there is general agreement, both in theory and in practice, that some New Testament writings are more important than others, that there is a hierarchy of authority among the various documents. Certainly the Gospels are more important than, for example, the Book of Revelation, and Paul's Letter to the Romans is more significant than the Third Letter of John.

The long and winding road taken by the New Testament followed the occurrence of the Church's foundational events. Although the Church originated without the New Testament, the Church without these sacred writings is now inconceivable.

To take so seriously, as this chapter does, the human and historical processes through which the New Testament came into existence does not mean that anyone should take the divinely inspired nature of these documents any less seriously. The New Testament reflects the historically and culturally conditioned mentalities of its many authors. But that is no reason to assume that whatever in the New Testament is out of sync with the times is more or less irrelevant. On the contrary.

"When the Bible disagrees with our modern times," wrote Scripture scholars James Turro and Raymond Brown, "it is not always because the biblical authors are giving voice to a limited, out-of-date religious view; frequently it is because God's ways are not our ways."[7]

Constantine's shift of the center of the Empire to the East prepared the way for the future split in the Church between Rome and Constantinople as the centers of the Roman Catholic and Eastern Orthodox Churches. The Constantinian era was a time of upheaval and change for the Church. It was, to echo Dickens, the best of times, the worst of times, a season of light and a season of darkness. It was, in other words, a time very much like the present and laden with lessons for the present.

CHAPTER 4

The Constantinian Era

O ne of the most significant moments in the history of the Church was the legalization of Christianity by the Roman emperor Flavius Valerius Aurelius Constantinus (280–337). Prior to Constantine's declaration that Christians were free to worship according to their beliefs, to become a Christian was, literally, to declare one's willingness to die for one's faith. Much of the story of Constantine is, however, lost in the mists of legend, so it is difficult to discover the exact historical details.

Constantine was born in Naissa, in Mesia (today, Nis, in the former Yugoslavia). His mother, Helena, was a Christian. His father,

Constantius Chlorus, who was tolerant toward Christians, became emperor of the Roman Empire's Western provinces in 305 and a member of the Tetrarchy, a system of two senior and two junior emperors begun by the emperor Diocletian in 293. Constantius died in 306, and his military leaders declared his son, Constantine, emperor. At this time he would have been twenty-six years old.

Soon thereafter, political chaos broke out. The Tetrarchy system of leadership collapsed. Seven claimants, including Constantine, began a struggle for power. On October 28, 312, at the Milvian Bridge, which spanned the Tiber River to the south of Rome, Constantine's army attacked Maxentius, his major rival in the West, and was victorious. About the same time, Licinius defeated his rivals in the East, and in 313 at the Convention of Milan, Constantine and Licinius agreed to divide the Empire between them. Constantine was to rule the Western provinces, Licinius those in the East.

The two emperors also agreed to declare complete religious freedom. Thus, the government returned all churches and cemeteries to their Christian owners without charge.

In the West, Constantine established laws that favored Christianity and showed an increasing regard for the dignity of the human person. Bishops were given the authority of civil judges if those in need of the legal services of the government so requested. Thus, Christians were allowed to free slaves in the presence of a bishop or, sometimes, in the presence of another cleric. Criminals are no longer to be branded on the face, said the authorities, because the human face is the image of God.

By 316 Constantine had abolished crucifixion as a form of execution, made concubinage (cohabitation without lawful marriage) illegal, and established laws protecting children. He also abolished laws that prohibited celibacy

In 321 Constantine issued an edict of special significance forbidding all work in the courts on Sunday, a "venerable day," and in 323 an official decree called the old religion "superstition." Also in 323, a new law said that anyone who forced a Christian to participate in pagan worship should be flogged or given a heavy fine. The emperor decreed that any Roman citizen in his will could leave money or property to the Church, and Christian symbols began to appear on official coins.

Constantine did not himself become a model Christian. Indeed, it is a fact that he ordered the death of his father-in-law, three brothers-in-law, a son, and his wife!

All the same, the new laws are evidence that Constantine, for whatever reasons, was influenced by Christian ideals. He tended to draw on the moral and religious values of Christianity and the authority of Church leaders for the good of the state.

In the Eastern provinces, however, Licinius was not so wholehearted in his support for Christianity. After 320 he began to harass the Christians under his rule. Licinius forbade Christian worship in towns or in enclosed places, and he required separate services for men and women. He made it illegal for the clergy to instruct women in Christian doctrine and harassed Christians who wanted to be charitable to those in prison.

Licinius dismissed Christians from his army and from government administrative posts, and he denied bishops permission to assemble for meetings. In some places, he closed or demolished houses of worship. Licinius arrested some bishops, banished others, and even executed a few.

In the summer of 324, war broke out between Licinius and Constantine. Licinius consulted the pagan oracles, while Constantine sent his army into battle under banners carrying a Christian sign. By September the war was over, and Constantine was victorious. Because Licinius's wife pleaded for her husband's life, at first Constantine spared him. He ordered that Licinius be held under detention in Thessalonica. Later, however, Constantine accused Licinius of plotting treason and had him executed.

With his victory over Licinius in 324, Constantine became sole ruler of the Roman Empire, and he decreed freedom of religion for the Eastern provinces as well. Constantine chose the city of Byzantium on the Bosphorus River, changed its name to Constantinople ("Constantine's town"), and made it the capital of the Empire and the center of the Roman government. The solemn consecration of the city as the new capital of the Empire was both pagan and Christian in character.

It is important to note, in passing, that Constantine's shift of the center of the Empire to the East prepared the way for the future split in the Church between Rome and Constantinople as the centers of the Roman Catholic and Eastern Orthodox Churches.

The key event in the life of Constantine was, of course, his victory over Maxentius at the Milvian Bridge in October 312. Historians know that after this event Constantine was openly sympathetic to Christianity. There are, however, no eyewitness accounts of Constantine's conversion. All the accounts that survive were written years or even decades later by dedicated Christians most interested in putting a Christian perspective on history. Thus one important question is: How historically reliable are the three literary accounts of Constantine's conversion to Christianity?

The learned bishop Eusebius, after 325 a powerful member of Constantine's court, wrote the earliest account, about the year 315, in his *Ecclesiastical History*.[1] This is the shortest of the three versions of the story and the only one to omit any mention of a dream or vision experienced by Constantine at the Battle of the Milvian Bridge. All the same, Eusebius states clearly that Constantine won his victory over Maxentius with the help of "God who is in heaven, and His Word, even Jesus Christ the Savior of all. . . ."

Then, said Eusebius, upon his triumphal entry into Rome, Constantine

> gave orders that a memorial of the Savior's passion should be set up in the hand of his own statue; and indeed when they set him in the most public place in Rome holding the Savior's sign in his right hand, he bade them engrave this very inscription in these words in the Latin tongue: "By this salutary sign, the true proof of bravery, I saved and delivered your city from the yoke of the tyrant; and moreover I freed and restored to their ancient fame and splendor both the senate and the people of the Romans.[2]

It is clear that Eusebius believed Constantine to have been a Christian, or at least convinced of the power of Jesus Christ, after his victory at the Milvian Bridge in 312.

The second account of Constantine's conversion, written by Lactantius, tutor of Constantine's son, Crispus, appears in a pamphlet Lactantius wrote, *On the Deaths of the Persecutors*.[3] This document, which most scholars date around 318, says that Constantine was instructed in a dream on the eve of the battle to place the "heavenly sign of God" on the shields of his soldiers.

> He obeyed and inscribed [the sign of] Christ on the shields: the [Greek] letter X intersected by the [Greek] letter I, bent at the top. Armed with this sign the army took up their swords.[4]

Lactantius says that Constantine's opponent, Maxentius, consulted "the Sibylline books," which told him that "on that very day an enemy of the Romans would perish." Taking this to indicate his own success, Maxentius "went out and engaged in battle." However, "the hand of God passed over the battlefield," and Maxentius went down to inglorious defeat; "pushed along by those fleeing, he was driven into the Tiber."[5] According to Lactantius, this

divine intervention marks the beginning of a
new era for the Church. From then on the purposes of Constantine and the purposes of the
Christian God would be identical.

The third and by far the most detailed
account of Constantine's conversion is in the
Life of Constantine, the authorship of which is
uncertain.[6] Loaded with miracles and divine
interventions, traditionally the *Life* is attributed
to Eusebius. More than a few historians, however, believe this document was written by an
unknown Christian author in the second half
of the fourth century.

A major problem with the *Life* is that it
claims to quote from documents that no longer
exist. Are these documents authentic? If not,
their historical value is subject to serious doubts.
This is no small point, for the *Life* is the traditional source for verifying the genuineness of
Constantine's conversion in October 312.

The key parts of the *Life of Constantine* are
the description of the miraculous vision and a
subsequent dream, the suggestion that the meaning of the vision was revealed to Constantine
by Christian interpreters, and the claim by the
author that he received his information direct
from the emperor himself.

According to the *Life,* Constantine was
uncertain as to which God he should pray to
for success in his battle at the Milvian Bridge.

He finally decided that he should pray to the God of his father, Constantius Chlorus, who appears here as much more of a Christian sympathizer than he really was. Constantine prayed to this God, asking for help.

> And while he was thus praying, a most marvelous sign appeared to him from heaven. . . . He said that about noon, when the day was already beginning to decline, he saw with his own eyes the trophy of a cross of light in the heavens, above the sun, bearing the inscription, "In this sign conquer." At this sight he himself was struck with amazement, as was his whole army . . . which witnessed the miracle. . . . And while he continued to ponder its meaning, night suddenly came on; then in his sleep the Christ of God appeared to him with the same sign which he had seen in the heaven, and commanded him to make a likeness of that sign . . . and to use it as a safeguard in all engagements with his enemies. . . .[7]

The *Life* gives a detailed account of how Constantine fulfilled this divine directive, and of how "God himself" assured him of victory.

Note that each subsequent version of Constantine's conversion story becomes longer and more detailed, and that the miraculous element, from being totally absent, balloons to epic proportions. The story says as much about the faith of those telling the story as it does about the event itself.

Three interpretations of Constantine's conversion dominated the work of historians since the nineteenth century. One says that Constantine was never a sincere Christian, that he only pretended to accept Christianity for political reasons. The second holds that Constantine considered the Christian God to be merely another member of his collection of gods, all of whom served to justify his claim to rule the entire Roman Empire. The third maintains that Constantine's conversion to Christianity was genuine and guided his religious policies as emperor.

According to Leo Donald Davis, S.J., most Church historians today believe that whatever sort of religious experience Constantine had prior to his victory at the Milvian Bridge in 312—the facts are lost in pious legend—after the battle he was sincere in his belief in the Christian God, though confused about what it actually meant.[8] Constantine gradually grew in his knowledge of Christianity, and was convinced that a common orthodox faith was necessary to a unified empire.

It is, however, a historical fact that for all his Christian sympathies Constantine was baptized only on his deathbed in 337. He then was buried in the Church of the Holy Apostles in Constantinople and to this day is venerated as a saint by the Eastern Orthodox Church.

The old pagan religion did not disappear overnight; indeed, in spite of official decrees, throughout Roman society it gave way to Christianity only gradually. Christianity's new-found freedom and its eventual acceptance as the official religion of the Roman Empire—in 380 during the reign of Theodosius, Constantine's successor—had, however, a dark side.

When it became the "in thing" to be a Christian, when there was no longer much risk in following Christ, it became difficult to distinguish sincere Christians from those baptized for form's sake. A secular government that smiles and approves of the Church can be as much of a threat to the Church's integrity as one that launches periodic persecutions.

In the words of Thomas Bokenkotter, "This alliance with the state profoundly influenced every aspect of the Church's thought and life. It carried many advantages, but it also entailed some serious drawbacks. . . ."[9]

The Church's freedom was compromised as government authorities exploited the relationship between Church and state for political purposes. Mass "conversions" were common when "going along" became the priority. Because members of the clergy received official status from the government, a virtual caste system developed in the Church, with clergy at the top and laity at the bottom. In more ways than one, after Constantine the Church would never be the same again.

Constantine is significant for more than just his role as the Roman emperor who legalized Christianity, however. For it was during Constantine's reign that the first of the great early Church councils took place, a council that was to have a profound impact on the life and thought of the Church down to the present day.

The First Council of Nicaea was called by Constantine, emperor of the Roman Empire, in late 324. This council lasted from about May 20 to August 25, in the year 325. Constantine, though not baptized and therefore certainly not ordained a priest, much less a bishop, thought of himself as *pontifex maximus*, "great pontiff," and "bishop in matters external." Some scholars suggest that Constantine believed he had authority to call such a council because as emperor he represented God on earth. At any rate, Constantine believed that he was responsible for facilitating the settlement of a dispute that, although religious in nature, was also a cause of division in the Empire. The central issue of the council was a heresy known as Arianism.

Nicaea, the site of the council, was in Bithynia, which today is an insignificant village called

Iznik, in northwest Turkey. Between two and three hundred bishops gathered in Constantine's palace, though later accounts gave the symbolic number 318, "the number of Abraham's armed servants in Genesis 14:14, a number which in Greek read TIH, symbol of the cross and Jesus."[10]

The bishops came from far and wide, some sympathetic to Arianism, others opposed. Some carried the scars of persecution on their bodies. One of the bishops was Nicholas of Myra, famous for his great charity, who would go down in history as Saint Nicholas and later as Santa Claus.

The First Council of Nicaea was no picnic. Prior to its opening, Constantine was inundated by written messages from the bishops, denouncing one another. All the same, the emperor opened the council with an address calling for peace and unity, and in front of all the bishops he destroyed, unopened, all the letters he had received.

The heart of Arianism revolved around the belief that the Word was not eternal with the Father. Actually, there was nothing unique about this belief, as many opinions existed prior to this time concerning the exact nature of the relationship between Jesus and God the Father. But it was Arius and his followers who brought the discussion to a head, and it was the religiously and politically disunifying strength of their consensus that demanded a response from both Church and State.

Arius himself attended the council, and Leo Donald Davis, S.J., describes him as "an elderly priest, tall, austere, ascetically dressed, grim of countenance, urbane in manner."[11] Though it is easy many centuries later to cast Arius in the role of a theological Simon Legree, it is impossible to deny that he and his followers were men of goodwill.

After no small display of verbal fireworks, the council condemned Arianism and accepted as the official creed of the Church the prayer now known as the Nicene Creed. This creed was based on an ancient Syro-Palestinian creed, but was modified to deny Arianism. Today, an adaptation forms a part of the liturgy of the Sunday Eucharist. The First Council of Nicaea originally worded the creed as follows:

> We believe in one God the Father Almighty, Maker of all things visible and invisible; and in one Lord Jesus Christ, the Son of God, begotten of the Father, only-begotten, that is, from the substance of the Father, God from God, Light from Light, True God from True God, Begotten, not made, of one substance with the Father, through whom all things were made.

Who for us men and for our salvation came down and became incarnate, and was made man, suffered and rose on the third day, And ascended into heaven, And is coming with glory to judge the living and the dead, And in the Holy Spirit.

But those who say, There was when the Son of God was not, and before he was begotten he was not, and that he came into being from things that are not, or that he is of a different hypostasis or substance, or that he is mutable or alterable—the Catholic and Apostolic Church anathematizes [condemns].[12]

While the Arians could live with "begotten from the Father" and "only begotten," they went cross-eyed with anger over phrases such as "from the substance of the Father" and "True God from True God," for these words plainly denied the Arian contention that the Son is a creature, not "co-eternal with the Father."

The phrase that really upset the Arians, however, was "of one substance [Greek, *homoousios*] with the Father," for these words clearly state that the Son shares the same being with the Father and is therefore completely divine.

Even though such a debate may draw polite yawns from the average Christian today, it is still a topic of great theological interest because the Arian brouhaha holds many implications for how believers understand who Jesus was and is.

A majority of the bishops at Nicaea, though they signed the final degree accepting the new creed and condemning Arianism, did not agree with some of the terms used to describe the relationship between the Son and the Father. The term *homoousios*, "of one substance," for example, had been used before by heretics, and it was not a scriptural word.

In the end, it took a threat of exile from Constantine to get seventeen holdouts to approve the creed. Arius and two of his followers were the only ones who still refused to sign, so they were excommunicated and sent into exile.

In spite of the controversy that surrounded its adoption and the fact that it did not receive unanimous approval by the bishops at Nicaea, the Nicene Creed was the first dogmatic definition of the Church, and it became a measure of orthodoxy down through the ages even to the present time.

The creed was the First Council of Nicaea's main accomplishment, but this council approved other forms of Church legislation, too. The council decreed that Easter should be observed on the Sunday following the first full moon after the spring equinox; that Jewish customs should not be normative for Christianity;

that bishops should be appointed by the other bishops of the respective provinces and approved by the metropolitan bishop; that clerics were to live only with women who were relatives or "beyond suspicion"—this applied only to celibates, for until about the eleventh century clerics were allowed to marry if they wished; and that on Sundays and the days of Pentecost people were to stand during the Eucharist, not kneel.

The First Council of Nicaea closed when Constantine confirmed its decrees and proclaimed them as laws of the Empire. He then wrote a letter to all bishops who were absent from the council expressing his joy that unity of faith had been accomplished.

This was the real world, however, and the Arian debate continued for many years after the council, and has continued to resurface in one form or another endlessly, it seems, which has its negative side to the extent that it may be unsettling to sincere believers, but it also has a positive, healthy side. For such theological debates serve constantly to inspire the People of God to reexamine and purify their belief, and to help them reaffirm its commitment to depend upon the love of God alone.

The Constantinian era was a time of upheaval and change for the Church. It was, to paraphrase Dickens, the best of times, and the worst of times, a season of light and a season of darkness. It was, in other words, a time very much like the present and laden with lessons for the present. Perhaps its central lesson is this: that change and theological debate have been a part of the Church's life from the earliest centuries, so Catholics should not be rattled by the fact that the same holds true today.

The Council of Chalcedon formulated a statement of faith inspired by Leo's *Tome* that, in effect, further developed what was contained in the Nicene Creed. This highly sophisticated theological statement is one of the most significant in the entire history of the Church.

The Council
of Chalcedon

No question is more central to Christianity than this one. Who and what was Jesus of Nazareth? Our response to this question affects virtually every aspect of Christian life and thought. If Jesus was only divine, then of what value are created realities, including humankind? If Jesus was only human, what good did he really accomplish?

If Jesus was God merely disguised as a human being, how can the Church claim that the realm of the human has a sacred character? If Jesus was simply a good and holy man, how can his brief presence nearly two thousand years ago make any difference today except as a "good example," however praiseworthy?

The Church's understanding of the trinitarian nature of God dominated its thought from the Council of Nicaea until the early fifth century. Gradually, however, a debate developed over how to explain the union of divinity and humanity in Jesus. How could Jesus be both the Word of God and Mary's child? The Word is eternal, but Jesus was "born of a woman" (Galatians 4:4), lived a human life, and died.

Two theological tendencies emerged, and the centers of these two schools of thought were Alexandria and Antioch. Theologians in Alexandria emphasized the unity in Jesus — that the Word who appeared in the flesh of Jesus was necessary for people to be united with God in love.

Antioch, on the other hand, insisted on the two aspects of Jesus' being, the human and the divine. Theologians in Antioch stressed the need to take Jesus' humanity seriously. This debate sowed the seeds for the great division between the Eastern (Orthodox) and Western (Roman Catholic) Churches, which exists to this day.

About 428, Nestorius of Constantinople attacked the popular piety that called Mary *Theotokos*, Mother of God. He insisted that this term was not in Scripture and that Mary could only be the mother of the humanity of Jesus.

Cyril of Alexandria opposed Nestorius and defended the unity of Christ. He argued that Jesus had a single nature and joined

Celestine, bishop of Rome, who condemned Nestorius in 430.

A theological uproar followed of such proportions that the emperor, Theodosius II, called a Church council at Ephesus in November 430 and asked all the provinces in the Empire to send a representative. He also invited Celestine. Note that smack in the middle of the fifth century Church councils are still being called by a lay secular ruler, not the bishop of Rome. In fact, Celestine was reluctant to attend because no bishop of Rome had ever done such a thing before.

Cyril of Alexandria arrived in Ephesus with blood in his eye; he would rid the Church of Nestorius if it was the last thing he did. Cyril, according to Church historian Jean Comby, "did not care what methods he used when his episcopal see and doctrine were at stake."[1] Therefore Cyril brought along some fifty Egyptian bishops who agreed with him, plus piles of gifts to give to sympathizers and to use along with a little arm twisting. Politics was the name of the game.

Cyril also was unconcerned when many of those invited to the council were not yet present on June 22, 431. Disregarding loud protests from the emperor's representatives and many bishops, Cyril opened the council on this date.

Socrates, an early Church historian, described the Council of Ephesus not long after the event. He wrote that it was held "immediately after the festival of Easter," and that "Nestorius [arrived], escorted by a great crowd of his adherents." Socrates then continues:

> When many had declared that Christ was God, Nestorius said: "I cannot term him God who was two or three months old. I am therefore clear of your blood, and shall in future come no more among you." Having uttered these words, he left the assembly, and afterwards held meetings with the other bishops who entertained sentiments similar to his own. Accordingly those present were divided into two factions. That section which supported Cyril, having constituted themselves a council, summoned Nestorius: but he refused to meet them, and put them off. . . .[2]

With Nestorius in a snit, off holding a council of his own, the Council of Ephesus examined Nestorius's public discourses and found him guilty of "distinct blasphemy against the Son of God."[3] In turn, Nestorius's council denounced Cyril.

Despite the great number of absentees, two hundred bishops accused Nestorius of being a heretic and called him a new Judas, not to mention many other unflattering names. "The crowd went wild with joy," writes Jean Comby, "and accompanied the bishops back to their lodgings with a torchlight procession."[4]

Now the story begins to take on the characteristics of a Shakespearean comedy. Onto the scene comes a bishop named John of Antioch, along with some other bishops who support him. John and his followers are angry at Cyril for his behavior, so they condemn Cyril, who retaliated by deposing John. In effect, everyone condemns everyone else.

But not quite. The emperor's representatives, true diplomats, now try to please everyone by deposing both Nestorius and Cyril. Cyril will have none of this, however, and escapes to Alexandria in triumph.

Now, however, Nestorius repents when he sees what a mess the situation has become. "So in bitter regret," noted Socrates, he called Mary *Theotokos* [Mother of God], and cried out: 'Let Mary be called *Theotokos*, if you will, and let all disputing cease.' "[5]

By now Nestorius's heart evidently was in the right place, but as far as Cyril was concerned, the damage had been done, so he banished Nestorius "to the Oasis, where he still remains. . . ."[6]

Meanwhile, Bishop John of Antioch has returned to Antioch and called together several other bishops who condemned Cyril of Alexandria. Soon, however, Cyril and John mended their fences, and "accepting each other as friends, they mutually reinstated each other in their episcopal chairs."[7]

But it was too late for Nestorius. "For the People were divided on account of . . . his unfortunate utterances; and the clergy unanimously anathematized [condemned] him."[8] Nestorius spent the rest of his life in exile.

The Council of Ephesus comes close to fitting Shakespeare's phrase, "sound and fury signifying nothing." The only official document issued was the condemnation of Nestorius. In effect, however, the Council of Ephesus reinforced the teachings from the Council of Nicaea and the emphasis on the unity of Christ. There would be no future dispute over calling Mary *Theotokos*.

Later, in 433, Bishop John of Antioch, still no friend of Cyril of Alexandria, proposed a theological formula designed to please all: "Union of two natures had been achieved . . . and because of this union we confess that the holy virgin is *Theotokos*, because the Word of God had been made flesh and been made man."[9]

Cyril responded that he accepted this wording, and the bishop of Rome sent congratulations to the two old adversaries when he approved John's formula.

Unfortunately, this agreement left the extremists on both sides with their noses still out of joint. Some continued to wave banners for the two natures in Christ, divine and human. Others claimed that in Christ the divine nature soaked up the human nature like a sponge. Still others insisted that Christ's body was not made of the same stuff, or substance, as other human bodies. Excommunications and condemnations flew like cudgels in the air.

Theodoret, bishop of Cyrus in Syria, continued to insist that in Christ there were two natures, divine and human, though he could not explain how the two were related to each other. Eutyches, a crotchety old monk who lived in Constantinople, claimed that in Christ the divine nature absorbed the human nature. For Eutyches, the human body of Christ was different from normal human bodies.

In 449 the emperor Theodosius II, who was a friend of Eutyches, called another council at Ephesus. Theodosius invited only supporters of Eutyches's position, not including Leo, the bishop of Rome, who believed that Christ had a real body of the same nature as his mother's and that his divine and human natures were united.

Among the friends and disciples of Eutyches was a bishop, Dioscoros of Alexandria, who brought a ragtag group of monks with him to Ephesus. And to compound the confusion, the representatives of Leo spoke only Latin, not Greek, so they could not make themselves understood and had hardly a clue as to what Eutyches and his followers were talking about.

This second council at Ephesus soon degenerated into pandemonium. Dioscoros of Alexandria shook his fists and denounced those who disagreed with him, and Leo's representatives furiously called for Dioscoros to be banished from the proceedings. Leo Donald Davis, S.J., describes what happened next:

> Pretending that he was being attacked, Dioscoros shouted for the imperial commissioner, who ordered the church doors thrown open. The provincial governor entered with the military police, followed by a motley crowd of monks, Egyptian sailors and assorted toughs. Flavian [patriarch of Constantinople] tried to cling to the altar, and, after being roughed up, managed . . . to find refuge in the sacristy. . . . Dioscoros forbade anyone to leave the church and despite anguished protests, all 170 bishops . . . signed the official acts. For greater convenience, some of the bishops were induced to sign blank sheets to be filled in later by Dioscoros' notaries. The main business of the council was complete:

Eutyches had been rehabilitated and restored; his accusers . . . deposed.[10]

When Leo heard about the goings-on at the Council of Ephesus, he was outraged and called the council a *latrocinium,* or synod of robbers. Leo then wrote a letter to the emperor insisting on his authority as bishop of Rome and, thus, as successor of Peter, to safeguard the truth. He also called on the emperor to convene another council to fight the injustices of the "robber synod." But Theodosius II was unresponsive and declared the issue settled. No slouch as a politician, however, Leo gained the attention of the emperor's sister, Pulcheria, and convinced her that his cause was a just one. As it turned out, Pulcheria was soon able to help Leo.

In July 450, Theodosius II, who had supported Eutyches, had been emperor for forty-two years and was no longer the equestrian he once was. He died after a fall from his horse while hunting. Soon thereafter, the new emperor, Marcion, married Theodosius's sister Pulcheria. She convinced him of the need for a Church council, but he decided that it would be better if the bishop of Rome was to preside at Church councils rather than the emperor. Therefore, he asked Leo to come to Constantinople to preside.

Leo declined, however, because Attila and his Huns were invading Italy and he thought it best to lie low. Besides, by now Leo was having second thoughts about the wisdom of calling a council. It was possible that the patriarch of Constantinople might try to grab more power for himself and so weaken the power of the bishop of Rome. But it was too late. Marcion insisted that a council be convened.

So Leo sent representatives to the council, which met first at Nicaea, but soon moved to Chalcedon, directly across the Bosphorus River from Constantinople. Thus, even though Leo was not present, this was the first time that a Church council had technically been presided over by the bishop of Rome. As things developed, it would later be unthinkable for a lay person, secular ruler or not, to call or preside at a council of the Church.

The Council of Chalcedon opened on October 8, 451, in the magnificent basilica of Saint Euphemia. Eighteen imperial commissioners had been sent by the emperor to keep an eye on the proceedings. Of the five hundred bishops present, not counting Leo's representatives, only two were from the West, and they were from Africa. Leo's men had places of honor to the left of the emperor's men, and they insisted that Dioscoros be seated among the accused.

The atmosphere was one of extreme tension; writes Thomas Bokenkotter, "cheers, imprecations, and groans burst out spontaneously as the proceedings unfolded."[11]

The trial of Dioscoros lasted into the night. Eventually, the evidence against him, showing by what underhanded methods he had gotten his way at Ephesus, was so overwhelming that all but twelve bishops abandoned him. Finally, Leo's representatives pronounced Dioscoros guilty, and they deprived him of his bishopric and the exercise of his ordination.

Next, once again the two old factions, those who favored one nature in Christ and those who believed in two, met in assembly with a copy of the Gospels set up ceremoniously between them.

A man with a loud clear voice stood up, waited for silence, and read the Nicene Creed, including the phrases added at the Council of Constantinople in 381, which emphasized the unity of humanity and divinity in Jesus. He also read aloud some letters written by Cyril of Alexandria and Leo's statement that divine and human natures were united in Christ. "He who became man in the form of a servant," Leo had written, "is he who in the form of God created man."[12] This was accepted teaching in the West and had been approved by such theologians as Tertullian and Augustine.

Leo's text, called the *Tome,* aroused much enthusiasm at the council. The bishops stood up and cheered: "This is the faith of the Fathers, the faith of the Apostles! This is what we all believe! Anathema [condemnation] on those who do not believe! Peter has spoken through Leo. . . ! This is what Syril taught! Leo and Syril taught the same thing!"[13]

Historians dispute whether the bishops at Chalcedon actually said, "Peter has spoken through Leo," but it is undeniable that by this time (the middle of the fifth century) the bishop of Rome had gained much prestige and power.

The Council of Chalcedon formulated a statement of faith inspired by Leo's *Tome* that, in effect, further developed what was in the Nicene Creed. This highly sophisticated theological statement is one of the most significant in the entire history of the Church:

> . . . we all with one voice confess our Lord Jesus Christ one and the same Son, the same perfect in Godhead, the same perfect in manhood, truly God and truly man, the same consisting of a reasonable soul and a body, of one substance with the Father as touching manhood, like us in all things apart from sin, begotten of the Father before the ages as touching the Godhead, the same in the last days, for us

and for our salvation, born from the Virgin Mary, the *Theotokos,* as touching the manhood, one and the same Christ, Son, Lord, Only-begotten, to be acknowledged in two natures, without confusion, without change, without division, without separation; the distinction of natures being in no way abolished because of the union, but rather the characteristic property of each nature being preserved, and concurring into one person and one substance. . . .[14]

In other words, the council taught that Christ is one person in two natures, and this became the measure of Christological orthodoxy in the Roman Catholic Church from that time to the present. Indeed, in the 1970s and 1980s Vatican authorities called a few Catholic theologians on the carpet for seeming to suggest ideas about Jesus contrary to the Chalcedonian definition.

Theologian Frederick J. Cwiekowski, S.S., explains the Chalcedonian doctrine this way:

The Council of Chalcedon taught that the humanity and divinity of Jesus were united in a single person (Greek: *hypostasis*). The word "person" was a philosophical concept, used to express the belief that Jesus, who was human and divine, was one individual, and not two. Human attributes, such as emotions, knowledge, the various capacities which enable one to reflect, to remember, to plan for the future, to make choices and decisions, were ascribed to Jesus because of his human nature. Divine qualities, such as being eternally one with the Father, having the power to forgive sins or to be an agent of creation, were ascribed to Jesus because of his divine nature.[15]

Church historian John C. Dwyer's interpretation is shorter and more concise. He writes that Chalcedon

> . . . reaffirmed that Jesus Christ is true God and true man, and that in him there are two principles of operation which remain distinct, but that there is only one acting subject, and that this subject is the divine Word.[16]

Among the difficulties related to the "one person in two natures" formula, however, is the fact that the language of Chalcedon is very technical and that language changes with history and human cultures.

How clearly can people understand what the Council of Chalcedon meant by its words? Do those words mean the same today? "As a matter of fact," responds John C. Dwyer, "they probably do not, and the result has been that Christians often feel obligated to speak of Jesus in a language which is alien to their world as it would have been to the world of the New Testament."[17]

It is unwise ever to forget that the Incarnation is the ultimate mystery of Christianity. It is impossible for the human mind to grasp this mystery; thus, human words can offer only analogies. These analogies are necessary, but they all limp. They reveal but they also conceal.

Perhaps tomorrow's Christians will have new words to better express their experience of the humanity and divinity of Jesus. These new words will need to not contradict Chalcedon, but they also will need to make sense to people of the twenty-first century.

The Council of Chalcedon did not bring peace to the Church. In fact, those who disagreed with Chalcedon announced that they would have nothing more to do with the Church that Chalcedon represented. The Monophysite churches upheld one nature in Christ, the Nestorian churches insisted on two natures.

It would be a mistake to overlook the role of politics in all this. When the emperor imposed the Chalcedonian doctrine upon all the territories in the Empire, many provinces rejected it in order to show their cultural and religious independence from the Greek culture of Constantinople.

Monophysitism carried the day in Egypt, where the language was Coptic, and in Syria, where the people spoke Syriac. In Syria the Monophysites adopted the Creed of Nicaea as modified by the Council of Constantinople in 381, to show their preference for a tradition older than what they regarded as the innovations of Chalcedon. Although the two situations have big differences, in a sense, the Monophysites were like Roman Catholics who rejected the teachings of the Second Vatican Council, which took place in the early 1960s, and announced that they would accept only the theology, traditions, and liturgy of the sixteenth-century Council of Trent.

Monophysitism and Nestorianism were adopted in other cultures, too, such as in Persia, where Nestorianism became the official religion in 486.

"As with the creed of Nicaea, one hundred and twenty-five years before," writes Leo Donald Davis, S.J., "the definition of Chalcedon was not the end but the intensification of a controversy."[18] Church and civil politics, as well as theological debates, combined to keep the pot boiling for many years.

Surely the most tragic outcome of this period of Church history happened thirty-three years after Chalcedon, in 484, when disagreement between the Eastern and Western Churches over Chalcedon's definition—the East charging that Chalcedon was a Nestorian council—resulted in a complete schism. It would be nearly four hundred years before the pope and the patriarch of the Eastern Orthodox Church would once again embrace. Even then the tragic schism would remain in effect.

For Pope Innocent III, the Church was virtually identical with the kingdom of God, so to extend the influence of the Church into the nations of the earth was to extend the kingdom of God on earth as well. The church/state divisions we take for granted today were completely foreign to the Christian perspective of the Middle Ages.

The Crusades, the Inquisition, Saint Dominic, and Saint Francis of Assisi

During the Middle Ages—roughly from the fifth to the thirteenth centuries—the Church faced major challenges, particularly in its relationship with society at large. The Crusades altered countless people's perceptions of Christianity. Saint Dominic and Saint Francis of Assisi inspired a new approach to preaching and living the gospel, and the Inquisition brought terrible discredit on the Church.

The Crusades

The Crusades were military efforts to regain control of the Holy Land, Palestine in particular, plus parts of western Syria and the eastern portions of the Byzantine Empire, all of which were under Muslim control. Christian soldiers went to fight "the infidels," their garments and banners decorated with the sign of the cross. These soldiers were, in Spanish, *cruzada*, "marked with the cross." Thus, they came to be called "crusaders."

There were three major crusades, plus a few minor ones. The first (1075–99) began when twenty thousand starry-eyed but totally unprepared peasants rampaged through Europe murdering Jews, after which they raped, pillaged, and plundered their way to Constantinople, the capital of the Byzantine Empire and the center of Christianity in the East. In Constantinople the crusaders destroyed the homes and churches of their fellow Christians, but when they reached Nicaea they met their match. Muslim troops slaughtered crusaders left and right and drove the rest back easily.

Later, in 1099, a second wave of some thirty thousand crusaders made it all the way to Jerusalem where they murdered seventy thousand men, women, and children. They then herded the city's Jewish population into the synagogues and burned them alive. This did not endear the Christians to either the Muslims or the Jews. That there may be bad feelings today on the part of certain Muslim countries toward the West, and Christianity in general, cannot be unrelated to historical facts such as these. We must also admit that the history of Christian antagonism toward Jews, and ultimately the death camps of Hitler during World War II, in which over six million Jews died, also have historical connections to the Crusades.

The Second Crusade began forty years later. Understandably, Muslim preachers rallied the various Muslim factions to unite against the invasions of "the Christian infidels." By now, both sides were calling the other side "infidels." Muslim troops took back Edessa in 1144, which the crusaders had captured during the First Crusade, and this infuriated western religious leaders.

Bernard of Clairvaux, the founder of the Cistercian, or Trappist, monastic order, was a mystic and a genius, but he was also a man of his own time. Bernard and the French king Louis VII called for a new crusade. Louis and

the German emperor Conrad III led this crusade, which turned into a fiasco. In 1148 the
crusaders were thoroughly defeated at Damas-
cus and returned home in disgrace, which
came as a major shock to the Christian West.
How could the "godless infidels" defeat the
armies of the true God and the true religion?

If the Second Crusade had not been such a
colossal failure, the history of the West might
have been different. Combined with the spirit
of independent thinking on the rise in the universities, the failure of the Second Crusade led
many thinkers to ask questions about the Christian faith and its supposed superiority. That
military force and religious faith are strange
bedfellows did not occur to these intellectuals.
For them, if God was active he would be active
in the military efforts of Christendom, and if
those military efforts failed maybe there was
something inadequate about the Christian religion. This line of thought seems strange to us,
but it made perfect sense even to the most sincere Christian believers in the twelfth century.

The Third Crusade began forty years later
when King Richard the Lionhearted of England,
Emperor Frederick I of Germany, and King
Phillip II of France decided once again to seize
the Holy Land from the Muslims. Off they rode.
Unfortunately, Emperor Frederick drowned on

his way east, and after conquering Acre (Ah-cray), north of Jerusalem, King Phillip grew tired of the whole business and went home. That left only King Richard. Anthony E. Gilles describes what happened next:

> When Richard beheaded 2,500 Moslem prisoners in Acre . . . Saladin [the Muslim caliph] responded by killing all of his English prisoners. In the ensuing battles the two rulers came to admire and respect each other greatly. Outdoing Western chivalry, Saladin once sent Richard a fresh horse during the height of a pitched battle so that the king could fight with his Moslem adversaries on equal terms. In 1192, having fought each other to exhaustion, the two sides signed a peace treaty which left Richard in control of a coastal stretch of land running from Acre to Joppa, but left Saladin in control of Jerusalem. Moslems and Christians were to be protected and tolerated in each other's territory.[1]

The Fourth (and final) Crusade owed its origins to the irritation felt by Pope Innocent III (1198–1216) because Jerusalem remained in the hands of "infidels." Innocent wanted to establish a Christendom under papal leadership that transcended national boundaries. That would include the Holy Land, of course, but it would also include a good many European countries as well. Naturally, the kings and emperors of European countries were not wild about this idea, so they sent their regrets when Innocent invited them all to another crusade.

Innocent's ambitions may sound unreasonable to us, but it is important to understand his perspective. For Pope Innocent III, the Church was virtually identical with the kingdom of God, so to extend the influence of the Church into the nations of the earth was to extend the kingdom of God on earth as well. The church/state divisions we take for granted today were completely foreign to the Christian perspective of the Middle Ages.

The Fourth Crusade went forward, but with mostly mercenary troops hired by the wealthy city-state of Venice and led by four French nobles anxious to lay their hands on the wealth of the East. To his credit, when Innocent III discovered the true motives of these nobles he declared that anyone who attacked Constantinople would be excommunicated from the Church.

The French nobles couldn't have cared less about being excommunicated, however. They showed Constantinople no mercy as their troops murdered, plundered, and raped at will. They even destroyed Christian churches and pilgrimage sites. This so-called Fourth Crusade brought complete dishonor on the crusades and destroyed forever the possibility of a reconcilation between the eastern and western churches. It also made it easier for Islam to tighten its grip on the East.

Four minor crusades followed in subsequent years, but they were equally futile. One of these was the tragic Children's Crusade. Thousands of children marched to the coast of Italy, on the Mediterranean Sea, in the belief that they would win back the Holy Land for Christianity by love rather than military force. Instead, hard-hearted, greedy merchants captured the children and sold them into slavery.

In the course of these lesser crusades, a German emperor actually gained control of Jerusalem for the West by negotiation with the Muslims. The pope, however, rejected the agreement because this emperor had been excommunicated from the Church. That's how seriously excommunication was taken at the time—by Church leaders, at least.

By the end of the thirteenth century, interest in crusades had died out completely. The Crusades accomplished the exact opposite of their intent. Muslim control of the Holy Land was solidified, and many westerners concluded that Islam had demonstrated its superiority over Christianity.

The Crusades were not without their good effects, however. The Crusades opened Europe to the East, even as far as China. Crusaders returned home with many wonders, including advances in astronomy, mathematics, and science. Many new inventions and ideas entered western society from the East. The crusaders brought back volumes of Greek philosophy preserved for centuries by Islamic scholars. All of this had a profound impact on European society, eventually leading to the Renaissance and such world-altering events as the French Revolution.

Saint Dominic and Saint Francis

During the years of the minor crusades, in Europe, especially in southern France, corruption was widespread among the clergy and in monasteries. Priests and monks lived a life of wealth and comfort and forgot about proclaiming the Good News of Jesus. This was a scandalous situation for countless ordinary Christians, one that inspired many to embrace poverty, simplicity, and self-denial.

A sect known as the Albigensians—from its origins in the town of Albi, in southern France—carried this to extremes, however. Members of this sect embraced a new version of an old Christian heresy, Gnosticism. The

Albigensians taught that the body and all material things are evil, which made marriage especially evil. Some members of the group went so far as to declare that life itself is evil, therefore the only way to liberate oneself from evil is to commit suicide. If everyone who bought into Albigensianism had agreed with this conclusion and followed through on it, of course, there would have been no more followers of the sect.

For some fifty years Church leaders tolerated the Albigensians. Finally, however, in the early thirteenth century Pope Innocent III decided to act on the old principle that heretics should be won over by reason not by force or violence. Innocent sent begging monks among the Albigensians to cast doubt on their assumption that the Church was completely corrupted by materialism. Unfortunately, this had little effect. A member of the Albigensian sect murdered a representative of Innocent III, and this prompted the pope to organize a military campaign against the Albigensians, sometimes called the Albigensian Crusade. This campaign was largely futile, however, so that twenty years later the pope—now Gregory IX—ordered what came to be known as the Inquisition.

Not to get ahead of ourselves, however, the begging, or "mendicant" monks—called "friars" from the Latin for "brothers"—Innocent enlisted were the followers of Dominic Guzman (1170–1221) and Francis Bernadone (1181–1226). These two charismatic leaders recognized the true spirit of evangelical poverty and simplicity found in the gospel, and they guided their followers away from the distortions of Albigensianism and the corruptions of the monasteries.

Dominic and Francis founded religious communities that took evangelical poverty seriously. Both of these communities also gave shape and form to a spirituality that had been quietly developing among ordinary people for many decades during the twelfth century. "The Dominicans and Franciscans," Anthony E. Gilles explains, "were not innovators so much as they were systematizers of an impulse toward the mendicant life-style which predated the births of Dominic and Francis."[2]

> These friars stayed on the move, teaching and preaching mostly in the growing towns, and they lived a simple life, dependent primarily on what people gave them for their efforts. . . . They had no farms for food or large monasteries for housing, at least not originally.[3]

The Order of Preachers, or Dominicans, founded by Saint Dominic, took preaching as their primary purpose. They wandered the countryside spreading the gospel to one and all, but they were especially concerned about countering the impact of the Albigensians.

The Franciscans took their inspiration from Francis of Assisi, perhaps the most popular saint of all time. The son of a wealthy silk merchant, Francis decided to live a life of poverty and take care of poor, sick, and needy people. Francis's father was not happy about this because he wanted his son to take over the family business. Francis responded that God was his only Father, and he even took off all his clothes in public and left them on the ground as a sign that he was shedding his old life in order to rely upon and serve God alone.

Pope Innocent III deserves considerable credit for approving both the Franciscan and Dominican orders. In the words of Church historian John Jay Hughes:

> Innocent opened the door to Francis and Dominic, men whom more conventional Popes would have considered dangerous innovators. To that extent we are justified in saying that the record of the friars, one of the great success stories of the medieval Church, must be counted among Innocent's greatest achievements.[4]

Not everyone appreciated the spirit of the Dominicans and Franciscans, however. Clergy and nobles alike felt threatened by Dominic and Francis and their followers, so they gradually imposed strict institutional rules and regulations on the two new communities. Before long, both the Dominicans and the Franciscans left behind the life of poor beggars and became highly educated scholars. Eventually, the papacy even began to use Dominican and Franciscan friars as instruments of the Inquisition: heresy-hunters. At this, Dominic and Francis were no doubt spinning in their graves.

The Inquisition

The men and women who later followed Francis found it virtually impossible to retain their founder's ideal of radical poverty, so the Franciscan order modified its rule without much argument when Church and civil authorities pressured them to do so. As scholars, Franciscan and Dominican friars were naturals for the Vatican to turn to when it needed men to counter heretical movements.

During the Middle Ages, take note, heresy was not just a wild bit of theological speculation that appealed to rebels and malcontents. "From peasant farmers to kings," wrote Carl

Koch, "the European Christians of the Middle Ages considered heresy a great evil. People feared that heresy would tear civilization apart and lead to eternal damnation for those people lured astray."[5]

Religion was not just a set of opinions about God, the meaning of this life and and the nature of the next life. Religion—particularly the Christian religion—was the glue that held society together. If someone threw around crazy religious ideas they could threaten the fabric of society itself. A heretic, therefore, was not merely someone with peculiar religious notions; a heretic was a traitor to the state, a person guilty of treason. Therefore, it made sense to take drastic measures to protect society from religious heretics.

Originally, until about the year 1150, civil authorities alone took responsibility for identifying and prosecuting heretics. A suspected heretic could be tortured until he or she agreed to give up all heretical beliefs. Sometimes heretics were burned at the stake or hung.

After 1150, local bishops could organize their own Inquisitions (the word means "inquiry"). If a bishop found someone guilty of heresy, he could ship the heretic off to the local civil authorities for punishment or execution. Archbishop Albert of Magdeburg, in eastern Germany, announced:

Anyone who has been convicted of heresy by the bishop of his diocese must immediately, upon the bishop's demand, be arrested by the secular judicial authority and delivered up to the pyre. Should the judges mercifully spare his life, he must at least suffer the loss of his tongue, by which the Catholic faith has been assailed.[6]

In 1252 Pope Gregory IX decided to have an Inquisition of his own. Gregory had in mind an effort to identify heretics, then talk the persons into giving up heresy. This Papal Inquisition actually dealt with people in a more just manner than the earlier civil inquisitions. Whereas local civil authorities would condemn a person without a trial, in theory, at least, the Papal Inquisition required a fair trial. The trial of an accused heretic took place in the presence of a papal representative, called an "inquisitor." Sometimes a jury would be gathered as well.

The Papal Inquisition occurred mainly in southern France, northern Italy, and certain sections of northern Spain. When an Inquisition was to be held in a town, Church officials would arrive and any suspected heretics would be called in to confess their heresy and receive a penance, or punishment. This would consist of reciting prayers, fasting, making a pilgrimage, paying a fine, . . . or being flogged.

If a heretic refused to give up his or her heretical beliefs, he or she could be imprisoned for life or executed by being burned at the stake. Both the trial and the execution were held in public. Sometimes, however, an execution would be delayed for as long as a year to give the heretic every chance to change his or her mind. In fact, relatively few executions took place. Hollywood and popular opinion give the impression that heretics were tortured and burned at the stake by the thousands, but this simply is not true. Even the most severe inquisitors rarely had anyone executed or even flogged.

People were naturally terrified of the Inquisition, although many believed it was necessary for the good of society. It was not unusual for someone to report someone else for heresy, but the possibility was remote that such a person would be tortured or executed.

For the most part, the Inquisition lasted only until the end of the thirteenth century, except in Spain where it lingered for some time longer — hence the awful reputation of the Spanish Inquisition, a reputation that continues to our own era. Today we look back on the Inquisition as a scandalous blotch on the history of Christianity. From our modern perpective, it strikes us as a terrible violation of human rights, to say the least. Understandable in its own historical context, through the Inquisition the Church learned that even it could be tempted to rely on violence to solve its problems.

It wasn't until the early sixteenth century . . . that an event occurred convulsing the Church so seriously that it actually resulted in the division of the Western Church and the birth of a major new Christian tradition. Between 1518 and 1555, many centuries of Christian unity in the West ended with the emergence of one man, Martin Luther, who sparked a movement that first was intended simply to call for reform but ended by cleaving the Church in two.

The Protestant Reformation

Conflicts and divisions were a part of the Church's life virtually from the beginning. During the public ministry of Jesus, his disciples argued about how money should be spent, and one of them gave up on Jesus and betrayed him. Some early Christians insisted that before one could be a Christian one first had to become an observant Jew.

During the early centuries of the Church's existence, theological controversies led heretical groups to split off from the main body of the Church. Rome and Constantinople divided over theological differences and over how to interpret conciliar teachings.

It wasn't until the early sixteenth century, however, that an event occurred convulsing the Church so seriously that it actually resulted in the division of the Western Church and the birth of a major new Christian tradition. Between 1518 and 1555, many centuries of Christian unity in the West ended with the emergence of one man, Martin Luther, who sparked a movement that first was intended simply to call for reform but ended by cleaving the Church in two.

The most natural question to ask about the Protestant Reformation is: What caused it? In broad terms, the Reformation was caused by the breakdown of the medieval social and cultural order and the gradual emergence of new attitudes and social institutions appropriate to the new order. Similar to the modern era, this was a time characterized by a better informed laity no longer comfortable with blind obedience to authority, whether secular or sacred.

It is a simple fact that the Church of the fourteenth and fifteenth centuries was corrupt, and it was corrupt from the top down. It also is a simple fact that if Rome had lent a more sympathetic ear to the legitimate concerns of Martin Luther and his followers the Reformation might never have happened.

On the one hand, there were bad popes and widespread abuses of clerical power. On the other, however, Church leaders failed to respond to emerging circumstances and perspectives and the demands of a new epoch. Unlike the Church of the early 1960s, which, albeit belatedly, saw the dawn of a new world and faced up to it at the Second Vatican Council, the Church of Luther's time saw the future coming and buried its head in the sand. At every level of Church life there were chaos and decay.

The papacy had moved away from a balance of power with the governments of secular states and was trying to grab more secular political power. "The papacy," wrote Church historians Iserloh et al., "seemed no longer to consider the interests of the Universal Church but all the more to be exploiting the nations of Europe in a thoroughly organized fiscal system."[1] In other words, money and more of it was the ultimate concern in Rome, not the Gospel and the spiritual health of believers.

Simony—the sale of Church-controlled positions, privileges, and property by the Vatican Curia to the highest bidder—was a taken-for-granted part of daily life. The Curia had at least two thousand jobs for sale, and a man could even become a cardinal for the right price.

During the decades just prior to the birth of Martin Luther in 1483, an intense struggle took place at the highest levels of the Church between those who favored conciliarism, a view that placed the ultimate authority in the hands of Church councils, and those who preferred power remain with the papacy. During these decades, the popes tried to protect themselves against democratic currents by agreements with secular governments. In this way they could avoid the embarrassing need for Church reform by bolstering themselves up with secular political power.

At the Council of Basel in 1431, Pope Martin V had to cough up much money to be recognized by the German princes, the emperor, and the king of France. He also had to relinquish much power over the Church to secular rulers, including the power to appoint bishops—for a price, of course.

The natural outcome of such papal groveling before secular powers was that in the course of the fifteenth century, instead of popes stressing their proper religious role in the face of secularization, they became more and more secular powers themselves. Emperors, kings, and princes looked upon the popes simply as other rulers to court as allies or oppose on the battlefield.

So entangled in this mess was Pope Leo X (1513–21) that he is sometimes called the savior of the Reformation, because he neglected for two years to give a serious response to Martin Luther's call for Church reform.

During the Middle Ages a powerful clericalism took hold that was rooted in a clerical monopoly over the schools and in the many secular privileges given to clerics. Priests and bishops forgot the example of their Master, who insisted that leadership is a service, not an excuse for lording it over others. The laity began to resent the clerical condescension and paternalism that went with all this, and their resentment contributed no little bit to the welcome Luther and his ideas received from the common people.

The time came when laity were beyond paternalism and were ready to function as mature adults. When this time arrived, it was the clergy's cue to relinquish control of secular matters and return more fully to their religious mission. Unfortunately, this did not happen.

"The Church," wrote Iserloh et al., "maintained outdated claims, and the world—the individual as well as the state and society—had to extort its autonomy. . . ."[2]

There were many personal abuses, too, among the clergy during the decades prior to the Reformation, including a widespread moral relativism, uncertainty about dogma, and priests and bishops who flaunted the discipline of celibacy by engaging in what a later century's sociologists would call "cohabitation." If marriage was forbidden them, they simply would not bother with the formalities.

As mentioned above, however, the corruption in the Church was from the top down.

Pope Leo X neglected his duties without a blush, preferring to party and have a good time. He is famous for his remark, "Let us enjoy the papacy since God has given it to us."

In the words of Church historian Anthony E. Gilles, "Leo epitomized all that was wrong with the Church on the eve of revolution. At age eight he had become an abbot. By the age of 13 he had been absentee bishop or abbot of sixteen benefices [dioceses, or monasteries acquired for the money they generated through taxes]. At 14, he was made a cardinal, and at age 37, still unordained, he was elected pope. He then proceeded to spend the equivalent of $25 million on his papal inauguration."[3]

Whatever credibility the papacy still had when Leo X assumed the throne of Peter, it was completely gone by the time he left it.

Pope Adrian VI, who succeeded Leo X in 1521 and knew by that time that the jig was up and that Church reform was unavoidable, said: "Depravity has become so taken for granted that those soiled by it no longer notice the stench of sin."[4]

The Church appeared to be the property of the clergy, meant to put money in the pockets of priests and bishops to support them in the high style to which they had become accustomed.

It is not as if Martin Luther was the first to call for Church reform. Far from it. For one hundred years prior to the Reformation, people had called for reform but their words had fallen on deaf ears. As early as 1455, Dietrich von Erbach, archbishop of Mainz, Germany, drew up and sent to the Vatican a list of German grievances against the papacy. In fact, he repeated this many times but got no response. And since nothing happened, the resentment of the German laity against the papacy grew more and more deeply entrenched.

Abuses seemed to touch every aspect of Church life, including the Mass. It was common to ordain poorly educated, even superstitious men and set them to work doing nothing but saying one Mass after another, for the money people would pay to have Masses said for deceased relatives. Thus, the Mass became an external ritual with no inner meaning, as if it were a kind of magic. In some German cities, so-called Mass priests constituted as much as 10 percent of the population.

The religious orders were in bad shape, too. Monasticism was at an all-time low, with community life and communal prayer virtually nonexistent. A few Cistercian monasteries seem to have maintained some semblance of virtue and integrity, but many Benedictine communities were completely out of touch with the spirit of their founder. Countless monks received permission to live outside their monasteries, and those who stayed often owned as personal property the "cells" they lived in.

The state of the mendicant orders—the Dominicans and Franciscans, who had so much responsibility for day-to-day pastoral care—would have given their founders, Saint Dominic and Saint Francis, apoplexy. "Monks and friars," wrote Thomas Bokenkotter, "were favored targets of satirists; according to a popular proverb of the day, one would do better meeting a robber than a begging friar. A famous anonymous satire, *The Letters of Obscure Men,* and the writings of Erasmus [a priest and scholar and one of the greatest men of this era] show that many people regarded the sons of Francis and Dominic as a pack of indolent ignoramuses. Nor was such an opinion merely the stock in trade of the perennially cantankerous and disaffected intelligentsia; the same views are found among the most loyal Catholics—people like Ignatius Loyola and Thomas More."[5]

Ultimate responsibility for the Protestant Reformation was as much the responsibility of the popes of the late Middle Ages as the result of Luther's teachings. Many Church leaders were aware of the state of the Church and the crying need for reform, but they could get no action from Rome. The popes were more interested in being secular politicians than spiritual leaders. Indeed, says Bokenkotter, between the late 1400s and early 1500s the popes "wallowed in corruption. . . ."[6]

It's not as if there weren't any good and virtuous Christians. Other reform attempts were made by religious orders, lay organizations — such as the Brethren of the Common Life, to which Thomas à Kempis, author of a timeless classic on the spiritual life, *The Imitation of Christ*, belonged — the secular clergy, secular princes, and scholars, notably the great Erasmus of Rotterdam (d. 1536), who agreed with much of what Luther said but refused to leave the Church. So concerned was Erasmus about the need for reform in the Church that a later Catholic wag quipped that Erasmus "laid the egg that Luther hatched."[7]

In the end, the Protestant Reformation happened because none of the reform movements could reach far enough — namely, to the point of reforming the papacy itself. Only with the Council of Trent (1545–63) would the papacy succumb to such efforts.

What made the Reformation occur when it did was the coming together of the right historical conditions and one man, Martin Luther, whose critique of the Church and its leaders struck a chord with the common people that continues to vibrate to this day. So significant is

Luther in the history of Christianity and of Western civilization that in the major libraries of Europe and the United States there are more books about him than about any other historical figure except Jesus.[8]

Martin Luther came from a lower-middle-class family. Born November 10, 1483, in Eisleben, Germany, he was the son of a hardworking father, Hans Luder, who labored in the copper mines and was a respected leader in the community. His mother was a sturdy but warm housewife of whom Luther spoke fondly in later years. Hans Luder moved his family to Mansfeld the year following Martin's birth. Martin's father was successful enough financially to be able to send his son to good schools where, however, a stern piety predominated, and Martin learned to fear God.

In 1497, at the age of fourteen, Martin went to a school in Magdeburg, and the following year to one in Eisenach. In both cities he had to earn his bread, according to the custom, by being an itinerant singer.

In the summer of 1501, Luther entered the University of Erfurt and began the basic course in the liberal arts. He won his bachelor of arts degree in 1502 and his master of arts degree in 1505. Fulfilling his father's wishes, his next step was to begin a study of the law, which he did on May 20, 1505.

On June 20, however, an event took place that would change not only Luther's destiny but also the entire course of European history. Luther went home for a vacation, and while he was returning to Erfurt on July 2, a tremendous electrical storm occurred at Statternheim, near the village. Lightning struck so close to Luther that it knocked him to the ground. He was so startled and frightened that he cried out, "Saint Anne, help me and I wil becomea monk!"[9]

Surviving the electrical storm and being at this time in his life not above a touch of superstition, excessive religious guilt, and spiritual legalism, Luther determined to keep his promise. Accordingly, he notified his father of his intention to enter a monastery, and although Hans Luder was less than happy about his son's sudden decision, Martin trotted himself off two weeks later to the monastery of the Hermits of Saint Augustine of the Observance in Erfurt.

After one year as a novice, Martin Luther took religious vows in September 1506. Just six months later, on April 3, 1507, he was ordained a priest. Little did the ordaining bishop realize that when he laid his hands on the young monk's head he touched the one who would become the source of the greatest religious, social, and cultural revolution in European history.

Luther completed studies in biblical theology and received his doctorate in 1512. The following year he was appointed to the chair of biblical theology at the University of Wittenberg.

Martin Luther's personal spirituality was not what anyone could call balanced. He was deeply fearful of eternal damnation and seriously in doubt as to the possibility of redemption. What Luther felt most of all toward God was fear, even terror. Thus, he expended much effort eking a resolution to his problem of how to be assured of salvation.

At some time after his move to Wittenberg, possibly in 1517, Luther found the answer he had been desperately seeking in Paul's Letter to the Romans, chapter 1, verse 17: "For in it [the Gospel] is revealed the righteousness of God from faith to faith; as it is written, 'The one who is righteous by faith will live.' "[10]

This was Luther's "eureka experience." He realized in a flash that one is acceptable to God because of what God has done for the sinner in Christ. Luther saw that the only task of the believer is to trust in God's acceptance in spite of sinfulness. "This insight," wrote John C. Dwyer, "brought [Luther] the peace which he sought and he was consumed by the desire to share his peace with others."[11]

Luther had searched for peace of mind and heart in the traditional practices of monastic life and in the sacraments of the Church, especially in a rigid and scrupulous approach to the confession of sins, but in the end it was in his private encounter with God in Scripture that he found peace. This fact is far from insignificant, for this was a highly individualistic experience, and it greatly relativized for Luther the role of the Church in one's relationship with God.

Indeed, it would not be misleading to say that some of the major themes in Luther's later theological writings can be traced to this one highly important personal religious experience. In Scripture Luther found a basis for condemning the corruption that afflicted the Church of his time. Salvation, he concluded, comes from faith alone.

The final straw for Luther came in 1517 when a young nobleman, Albrecht of Brandenburg, decided that he wanted to be archbishop of Mainz, which would make him the most important man in the Church in Germany. To become archbishop would, however, require much money to buy the position from the pope, the corrupt and frivolous Leo X. And the curia would jack the price up even higher than usual because Albrecht would need to buy a dispensation for being too young to hold the office.

Albrecht took out a gigantic loan to pay the fees demanded by Rome, which left him with the problem of how to repay it. What to do, what to do? Albrecht hit on the idea of preaching to the people a special indulgence whereby they could free the souls of dead relatives and friends from purgatory. The preaching would give lip service to the need for good works, also, but without money good works would be worthless.

The pope, who needed money himself to complete construction on Saint Peter's Basilica, readily approved the deal with Albrecht. The word the young nobleman gave out to the public was that the money collected would be used to finish Saint Peter's. On the sly, however, the curia had agreed to split the take with Albrecht so he could drag himself out of debt.

Johannes Tetzel, a Dominican friar, was appointed to promote the indulgence by preaching in Wittenberg and other parts of Saxony. Unfortunately, if anyone had gone looking for the least qualified preacher they could find, they could not have done better than Tetzel. His theology could not have been worse. Tetzel announced that when a person dropped some money into the collection box to pay for the indulgence, the soul of the dearly departed would at that very instant spring from the purgatorial fires into heaven.

Luther saw red when he heard what Tetzel was saying. So, on October 31, 1517, he sent his famous Ninety-five Theses, or theological statements, written in Latin, to the bishops in the areas where Tetzel was active. Legend has it that Luther marched indignantly up to the church in Wittenburg and nailed his theses on the great wooden doors. In fact, however, for all the dramatic value of this image Luther probably did not do this. And even if he did, it would have been no big deal, as people did that sort of thing all the time. The doors of the local church were used as a kind of community theological bulletin board.

When Luther sent his Ninety-five Theses to the bishops on his mailing list, complaining about the sale of indulgences, he had no intention of making them public. However, once someone "leaked" them to the public and they were translated into German and given a wide distribution, they captured the popular imagination. It is from this time that the Reformation is dated. It is important to remember, however, that at this point nothing was further from Martin Luther's mind. His sole intention was to reform the Roman Catholic Church.

Albrecht, whose money-raising project Luther had just shot down, was not pleased. In fact, he was furious, so he complained to Rome, and the following year, 1518, the curia started the process to determine if Luther was a heretic.

In October 1518, at the Imperial Assembly in Augsburg, Cardinal Cajetan, probably the most brilliant theologian of the time, demanded that Luther abandon his theological positions. Luther refused, and under cover of night he slipped out of Augsburg.

Luther petitioned Rome to call a Church council, but this suggestion only caused Leo X and his advisers to become anxious, because anything might happen at a council, and this was too much of a threat to the status quo.

Subsequently, Luther agreed to a public debate, which took place during June and July 1519. Luther's opponent was Johannes Eck, a professor of theology at the University of Ingolstadt.

Luther admitted, in the course of the debate, that he did not accept the authority of the pope or of Church councils. For Luther, whose personal moment of salvation came in a solitary encounter with a passage in Paul's Letter to the Romans, the only authority was Scripture.

"Eck," wrote John C. Dwyer, "was sincere and a clever debater, but it is impossible to read the transcript of the debates without concluding that it was Luther who had real religious substance on his side, even though some of his views were dangerously one-sided, and that Eck was defending some practices and views of the late medieval church which were doubtfully Christian."[12]

Beginning in 1520, the juggernaut that was the Protestant Reformation really began to roll.

Luther's writings, aided by the invention of the printing press, circulated far and wide. Luther proclaimed the priesthood of all believers and the priority of councils over popes. He denied that the Mass was a sacrifice and rejected all the sacraments except Baptism and the Eucharist, saying that none of the other five had any basis in Scripture. Luther also wrote that good works do not make a person good. Rather, good works are the expression of the saved person.

Luther's writing style was lively and captivating, unlike the dusty-dry style of the average academic of the time, so people enjoyed reading what he wrote. As time went by, Luther became a folk hero, what today would be called a celebrity. If *Time* and *Newsweek* magazines had existed then, Martin Luther would have been on the the front covers more than once.

Finally, in December 1520, came the gesture that symbolized Luther's final break with the Catholic Church. Luther publicly burned the papal document threatening him with excommunication.

If there is a single lesson in the story of Luther and the Reformation it may be this: It is naive in the extreme to think that Church leaders are above secular temptations, and it is sheer folly to ignore the need for the Church, in faithfulness to the Gospel, always to grow, deepen, and adapt itself according to the signs of the times while remaining faithful to the substance of the truth.

It was the Reformation that ultimately caused Church leaders to call a general council, at Trent, to deal with the need for reform and to respond to the Protestant challenge. Some would call it too little too late. Together, however, there is no question that the Protestant Reformation and the Catholic Church's response to it at the Council of Trent had a profound impact on the life of Catholics for the next five hundred years.

The Council of Trent contributed a great deal to the way the modern papacy took shape. Without feeling any need to justify such a perspective historically or theologically, it reaffirmed papal supremacy and submitted its decrees to the pope for approval. It also gave the pope the task of tying up loose ends that the council had not had time to resolve. Without explanation, the council gave the pope absolute, unrestricted power in the Church. In effect, Trent smashed a bottle of champagne on the bow of an autocratic papacy and cheered it down the slips and into the waters of modern history. This fact would have tremendous repercussions in the centuries to come.

CHAPTER 8

The Council of Trent

Common opinion says that the Council of Trent (1545–63) was purely and simply the Catholic Church's response to the Protestant Reformation. Such opinion takes for granted that the split within Christendom was final and irrevocable when Trent convened and that the Church's only option was to circle its wagons and prepare to fight off the Protestant heresies. Reality was not, however, quite that simple.

Certainly the process that would lead to such a final division was well under way. But it is important to note that if the Protestant reformers' efforts constituted the straw that broke the camel's back, for all the good it accomplished, the Council of Trent kicked the camel in the head when it was still possible for it to struggle to its feet again. In other words, Trent must accept some responsibility for the finality of the split between the Church and the Protestant Reformation.

In the words of John C. Dwyer:

> The problem of Trent was . . . that the pope and the bishops from the Latin countries identified Latin Catholicism, and its customs, its devotions, its whole religious ethos, with Christianity, pure and simple. They had been doing this for centuries with the Orthodox churches of the East, and it was a hard habit to break. The bishops of the southern lands were horrified when German Catholics, as well as Protestants, had asked for a married clergy and for the granting of the chalice to the laity. But if Latin Catholicism had been willing to yield on those two points (which touch only discipline and not faith) in 1525 or 1530, it is possible that genuine reform could have been achieved in one church.[1]

As the last chapter noted, the seeds of the Protestant Reformation were in the ground before Luther was born, and it is also true that there were reform efforts within the Church after Luther's bombshell. Still, it took twenty-eight years from the time when the currents of history carried Luther's Ninety-five Theses far and wide before the pope successfully called a general council of the Church.

Obstacles to a council, which delayed it for so long, included papal fears of a resurgence of conciliarism, which taught that a council had greater authority than a pope. There was intense opposition, too, from powerful members of the Roman Curia—the pope's "central administration"—who opposed a council because they believed reform would reduce to a trickle the flow of money into curial coffers. Secular rulers also opposed a council because they perceived such an idea as a political threat.

Still, even with all the good efforts of influential groups such as the Jesuits, any lasting reform needed to occur from the top down. The financial abuses, organizational chaos, and widespread doctrinal confusion that had characterized Church life for so long could be dealt with effectively only by a pope who was willing to spark reform beginning with the papacy itself.

The man who finally had the moxie to start the ball rolling was no saint, but at least he was willing to act. Pope Paul III, whose papacy lasted from 1534 to 1549, was a product of "the bad old days," the corruption and laxity that had permeated the higher levels of the Church for many years. Although never married, he was both a father and a grandfather, and two of his sons were highly placed through his influence. Still, he saw the writing on the wall and turned a deaf ear to those who whined and complained about how dangerous a council would be.

There was, of course, a variety of opinions among those who supported Paul III on exactly what sort of Church reform a council should seek. Some felt that only a major shakeup in the curia, the religious orders, and the diocesan clergy would do the trick. Others believed that a slow-moving, don't-rock-the-boat, gradual reformation of Church institutions and policies would be the most effective approach. As the French say, the more things change the more they stay the same.

Among those who opposed the pope, the conservatives, consisting mainly of curial legalists, insisted that reform could be accomplished by a strict return to a "law and order" approach to Church life. There were also those troglodytes, in this as in all eras, who in the face of any threat to the status quo, wrung their hands, danced nervously about, and cried, "Please, don't! We've always done it this way!"

For his part, Pope Paul III allowed the various factions to express themselves freely, without comment, which shows either that he was far more wily than many gave him credit for being or that his desire for reform had definite limits. It is likely that the latter is closer to the truth.

Paul III was not the first true reform pope, but he saw the need for reform, and he knew that a Church council was the only way to accomplish that goal. He also appointed honest, clear-eyed men to the curia and as cardinals who were reform-minded.

In the fall of 1536, Paul III asked eight men who had no debts to the curia, financial or otherwise—men who were known to be upright and independent—to come to Rome to study the question of Church reform. On March 9, 1537, this group handed the pope a document frankly stating that the root of the Church's problems was to be found in, so to speak, "elephantiasis of the papacy." The pope's power had grown completely beyond its proper bounds. Another serious problem was a rampant lust for money among bishops, cardinals, and curial bureaucrats.

The document called for reform of curial procedures in the granting of dispensations from various Church rules and regulations, greater attention to who was and was not ordained to the priesthood, and, in general, a return to a genuinely Christian spirit in Rome. In effect, this group of eight looked the pope in the eye and said, "Guess what, your Holiness, much of what Luther said is as true as the day is long."

Apparently because he was weak of knee, Paul III chose not to make this document public. Before long, however, he decided to convoke a general Church council. First, he announced that it would be held in Mantua, beginning on May 13, 1537. Various secular leaders squawked, however, so the pope switched the location to Vincenza. Political clashes frustrated this attempt, too, however, so on May 21, the pope announced that the council would be postponed indefinitely.

After a nonconciliar attempt at reconciliation with the Protestants failed, and after reports that Protestantism had penetrated Italian borders, Paul III in the summer of 1541 returned to the idea of a council. The emperor, Charles V, suggested Trento (Trent), in northern Italy.

Finally, the pope took the bull by the horns and, ignoring all nay-sayers, called the council to meet on the third Sunday of Advent, in Trento. Although the turnout was far from overwhelming—only four archbishops, twenty-one bishops, and five generals of religious orders showed up—the council officially opened on December 13, 1545.

The Council of Trent lasted eighteen years, but was in session for only a little more than three of those years. The first session (1545–48) ended when Emperor Charles V decided to try again to win Catholic-Protestant unity through dialogue and compromise, an attempt that failed. Ten years lapsed between the second (1551–52) and third (1562–63) sessions because political leaders during these years were less than enthusiastic about religious issues, and the successor of Paul III, Pope Paul IV (1555–59), preferred to take matters into his own hands. The next pope, however, Pius IV (1560–65), had more faith in the conciliar approach. Through shrewd diplomacy and hard work, he managed to reconvene the council for its final session.

Actually, between April 1547 and February 1548, the Council of Trent became the Council of Bologna, at least unofficially. An epidemic of typhus broke out in Trento, so the pope moved the council to Bologna. Although the council issued no decrees while in this city northeast of Florence, important debates took place there on the sacraments, the Mass, purgatory, the veneration of saints, and monastic vows.

No decrees were issued from Bologna, however, because Paul III didn't want to irritate the emperor overmuch. For while Trento was under the emperor's control, Bologna answered to the pope.

The emperor, Charles V, demanded that the council return to Trento, but Pope Paul III refused. Charles made a formal protest, which he sent to both Rome and Bologna. The pope's response was to suspend the council on February 16, 1548, which brought the first session to a close.

After the death of Paul III the following year, his successor, Julius III, gave in to pressure from the emperor and returned the council to Trento, where it opened again on May 1, 1551, although work did not begin in earnest until late that summer. Eventually, however, this session issued decrees based mainly on the work that the council had done in Bologna. The council was suspended again on April 28, 1552, because another war broke out.

In 1553 Julius III put together a lengthy document meant to deal with the need for Church reform, but he died before it was published. The next pope, Paul IV, opposed the council entirely, so he called a papal reform assembly in Rome in 1556 as a substitute. This did not work either because war erupted between the papacy and Spain.

Paul IV also revived the Inquisition, largely to deal with the Protestant heretics. Ironically, it took on especially horrible dimensions in Spain. In the words of Anthony E. Gilles:

> Perhaps in no other country was Paul's Roman Inquisition imitated as zealously as in Spain. The Spanish Inquisition, directed

principally against Jews and Moslems since the late Middle Ages, had become proverbial as an instrument of brutal oppression. . . .

By the time of Paul IV the Spanish Inquisition was led by a "Grand Inquisitor" who supervised 14 local Inquisitors. The tentacles of the Spanish Inquisition spread throughout Spain, becoming in effect the equivalent of our century's Gestapo or KGB.[2]

It took the successor of Paul IV, Pope Pius IV, and the popularity of Calvinism — named for a major Swiss Protestant reformer, John Calvin — in France to get the council back on track. But not without further complications. Some secular rulers wanted to start a completely new council; others wanted to continue the Council of Trent. With no official resolution of this argument, Pope Pius IV convened a council at Trento on January 18, 1563, and 113 bishops voted to resume consideration of the agenda that had been interrupted in 1552.

Still avoiding the question of whether this was a new council or a continuation of the old one, the council fathers discussed whether to require bishops to live in their dioceses. The scandal of "absenteeism" was great, but, incredible as it seems today, it took much hot debate before the council resolved to require bishops to do just that.

One of the most far-reaching decrees of the council was on marriage. Although motivated by good intentions, this decree had a profoundly dehumanizing, even un-Christian, effect on the Church's attitude toward divorce and remarriage for the next five hundred years. Dated November 11, 1563, Trent decreed that secret marriages—a serious problem at the time, because in such cases a man could easily abandon his wife and claim they had never been married—were both illicit and invalid. This decree made the validity of marriage dependent on the solemnization of the union in the presence of "the competent pastor" and two or three witnesses. Also, the marriage was to be recorded in a register.

For understandable reasons, this decree opted for a legalistic view of marriage. The council said nothing about the need for love between husband and wife in order for the marriage to be "licit and valid." Thus, for the next five centuries, marriage was defined in legalistic rather than personal terms, which made it difficult for anyone married before a priest and two witnesses to obtain an annulment of a marriage from the Church, regardless of how inhuman that marriage may have later become.

The issues of indulgences and veneration of the saints and relics had been hot topics ever since Luther denounced them in the midst of widespread abuse. Trent insisted that the Church has the power to grant indulgences; in other words, that there is a place of purification after death (purgatory), which the living may help the departed to get through by their prayers and good works. The council also insisted that veneration of the saints is good for a person's spiritual life and that to venerate the saints' relics is fine because one honors not the relic itself but the one whom the relic represents.

Trent answered each of Martin Luther's major criticisms of the Church. Luther said that Scripture alone is the source of Christian revelation. Trent said Scripture and Tradition. The council decreed that "the apostolic traditions on faith and custom that 'have been transmitted in some sense from generation to generation down to our own time' were to be accepted 'with as much reverence'. . . as Sacred Scripture."[5]

When the majority of the council fathers at Trent said "Tradition," however, they had in mind a material addition to Scripture, a body of material that could be collected and quantified. Today, on the contrary, the Church understands Tradition as the Church's ongoing experience of faith. The Bible itself is a product of Tradition. "'Sacred Tradition and Sacred Scripture,' then, are bound closely together and communicate one with the other," explains the *Cathechism of the*

Catholic Church, quoting the Second Vatican Council's 1965 document on divine revelation. "For both of them, flowing out from the same divine well-spring, come together in some fashion to form one thing and move towards the same goal" (no. 80; see Vatican II, *Dei Verbum,* no. 9).

"Before there were written texts," wrote theologian Richard McBrien, "the faith was handed on through proclamation, catechesis, worship, and personal example. For Catholicism, God speaks through means such as these, not only through words but through deeds as well. History in general and the history of the Church in particular are carriers of divine revelation. Catholicism, therefore, not only reads its Sacred Scripture, but also its own corporate life and experience."[4]

A second decree at Trent on the sources of revelation said that a revision of Saint Jerome's fourth-century Latin translation of the Bible, called the Vulgate, was to be the official Catholic version of the Scriptures. This did not mean that there should be no study of the ancient Greek and Hebrew texts. In effect, however, Trent did not go out of its way to encourage study of the Scriptures by scholars or the reading of the Bible by ordinary people. If the Protestants overemphasized the Bible and downplayed the sacraments, the Church would deemphasize the Bible and give much attention to the sacraments.

Luther said that justification, or salvation, came from faith alone. Trent said that faith must be joined by hope and love that express themselves in good works, all supported by the grace of God.

Encouraged in no small part by his interpretation of the writings of Saint Augustine of Hippo (354–430), Luther said that human nature is completely corrupt as a result of Original Sin. Trent said that we must leave at least a small bit of room in human nature for some basic goodness and freedom.

Luther insisted there are two sacraments only, Baptism and Eucharist, claiming that there is no basis in Scripture for the other five. Trent insisted on the traditional list of seven sacraments and defined sacraments as "efficacious signs, bringing grace by the rite itself . . . and not simply by reason of the faith of the recipient."[5]

The council reaffirmed the traditional seven sacraments: Baptism, Confirmation, Eucharist, Matrimony, Holy Orders, Penance (now often called Reconciliation), and Extreme Unction (now called Anointing of the Sick).

Against Luther, the Council of Trent also reaffirmed the hierarchical nature of the Church, the divine origins of the priesthood, and the teaching that in the Mass "transubstantiation" takes place. That is, that the invisible substance of bread and wine becomes the invisible substance of the sacred "body and blood"—a Semitic phrase that means "the whole person"—of the risen Christ. Thus, Trent preserved the profound mystery at the heart of the Eucharist. For only the heart, not the intellect, can truly embrace the reality of the risen Christ's loving gift of his very self in Holy Communion.

Trent also proclaimed, contrary to Luther, that the Mass has a sacrificial character. This means that the Mass manifests the sacrificial love of Christ's acceptance of his death on the cross.

Some today would offer the term *transubstantiation* as an example of how each new age requires a new explanation of the Christian mysteries, such as the sacraments. Does the word transubstantiation carry the same meaning for people on the threshold of the twenty-first century that it carried in the sixteenth century? Or has it become for most people, except professional theologians, a kind of theological password, with no basis in contemporary faith experience, which one must nevertheless use to prove one's orthodoxy?

One of Trent's most significant moves was the reform of the Mass, and the need was nothing short of spectacular. The medieval Mass had become a theatrical event with magical overtones. The priest said the Mass, and the people who attended were restricted to the role of spectators. There was virtually no sense of participation on the part of those in attendance, which was critical to the ancient Church's understanding of the liturgy.

Also, due to the hand-copying of liturgical books, a wide (and sometimes bizarre) variety of local liturgical oddities had come into existence. Individual priests felt free to give rein to their personal liturgical eccentricities—a quirky phenomenon not altogether absent from celebrations of the Eucharist today.

It was also common for priests to sell Masses, to be offered in a quasi-superstitious way on behalf of dead relatives and friends, for as much as the market would bear. Luther could not have been more correct in his opposition to such abuses.

In 1570 the council issued the *Revised Roman Missal* and proclaimed that all Masses in all places throughout the Church were to be celebrated only according to the letter of the Church's liturgical laws, called "rubrics," set down in the missal. It was this form of the Mass that became normative after the Church had been in existence for some fifteen hundred forty years, a form of the Mass very different from that celebrated in the early centuries of the Church.

The "Tridentine Mass" was used throughout Roman Catholicism for the relatively brief period of five centuries, prior to the liturgical reforms of the Second Vatican Council (1962–65). In the early 1990s Pope John Paul II gave local bishops permission to allow the celebration of this pre-Vatican II Latin Mass in their dioceses, if they wish to do so.

If anything is unfortunate about the form of the Mass that Trent made binding on the Church, it was its rigid character. There was no reason, for example, that the vernacular, the ordinary language of the people in the various parts of the world, could not have been used. After all, the Mass was originally celebrated in Latin simply because that was the language of the people in the Roman Empire.

Sadly, the main reason Trent insisted on the Mass in Latin was that to change to the vernacular would have been to admit that the Protestants were correct. Also the Council of Trent had a lack of historical perspective about its deliberations that kept the example of the early Church's liturgy from view.

In fact, writes Thomas Bokenkotter, the Tridentine Mass had both positive and negative implications:

The Tridentine Mass was tremendously effective in securing a uniform religious expression throughout the world. As a pedagogical tool for instilling the Catholic sense of tradition and emphasizing the clarity, stability, and universality of Catholic doctrine, it was superb. But on the negative side it helped to engender the myth of the unchangeable Mass, the sign and proof of the unchangeableness of the Roman Church (a myth whose overthrow has lately caused much confusion). And above all it failed radically to restore to the people a sense of participation—forcing them to run after a multitude of extraliturgical devotions in order to satisfy their need to feel involved in the worship of the Church.[6]

The Council of Trent closed on December 4, 1563, after a breathless messenger arrived with the news that the pope was on death's doorstep.

Two major topics that Trent neglected entirely were the nature of the pope's role in the Church and the nature of the Church itself, both of which were major points of contention with the Protestants.

To mix a couple of metaphors, in effect the Council of Trent called out, "Raise the drawbridge!" and "Batten down the hatches!" The council fathers focused on doctrinal confusion in the Church and on the breakdown of institutional structures. Although it never mentioned his name, each of Trent's decrees was a response to Martin Luther.

For the most part, and understandably so, Trent was a conservative council. It placed much emphasis on shoring up the various institutional structures of the Church. One result was that the parish became the unquestioned center of Catholic religious life. If there was any common understanding prior to Trent that religious experience could happen anyplace, after Trent the Church left no doubt that religion happened in the parish church.

If there was any sense before Trent that parents played a key role in the religious formation of their children, after Trent Catholics soon took it for granted that the parish priest was the one ultimately responsible for the catechetical formation of children, the clear implication being that in this respect the family was incompetent.

Church historian John Bossy suggests that following the Council of Trent the Church became implicitly antifamily. "The Catholic Church made a direct and conscious attempt to mold the Christian as an individual in a parish context, instead of as part of family, kin and social networks."[7]

For example, Church legislation on baptism and confession had a negative effect on family life. The Church required that an infant be baptized within three days of birth, which left little if any time to assemble the extended family. This requirement separated baptism from the family welcoming celebration and emphasized that salvation is an individualistic concern. Further, although previous custom had allowed for many godparents, including young children, which created a bond among members of the extended family, Church law following Trent limited godparents to one male and one female.

During the post-Tridentine Counter-Reformation period, Charles Borromeo introduced the confessional box, privatizing the sacrament of Confession. He might as well have proclaimed that salvation, repentence, and sin were private matters with no wider social implications. Reconciliation was no longer recognized as essentially public or quasi-public, and so no longer a matter for family and the wider community.

Church historian David Herlihy supports Bossy's thesis. Following Trent, he says, wives were encouraged by preachers to inform the parish priest if their husbands became involved in any activities that could be taken as other than consistent with official Church rules and regulations.

For centuries prior to Vatican II, many religious orders refused to allow their younger members even to visit the homes of their parents, for the "secular home" was no place for a "sacred Religious." This sacred/secular dichotomy relegated the family home to a secular status. In other words, in the past the Church used families as its prime source for religious vocations, but it did little in return to empower families.

Prior to the Counter-Reformation, which followed in the wake of the Council of Trent, family religious customs were more central to Catholic religious practice than what went on in parishes. The Counter-Reformation, however, set firmly in place the notion that the parish was the core of Catholic faith life.

All this raises the question of whether the Church, after Trent and before Vatican II, had institutionalized antifamily biases. In some respects, at least, it seems that the answer is yes. Today, however, the words of Pope John Paul II give a clear indication of the attitude that should dominate in parishes today: "No plan for organized pastoral work must ever fail to take into consideration the pastoral area of the family."[8]

Not until Vatican II would Catholics begin to recover the ancient Church's conviction that the family in its various forms, not the parish, is the most basic unit of the Church and that parents are the primary religious educators of their children — not in a formal or academic sense, of course, but in the sense that parents form their children in countless informal ways every day.

The Council of Trent required seminary training for future priests, a training that would take on a heavily monastic, antifamily tone in the centuries following the council. It also paid little heed to developments in Scripture studies. Thus, the notion that marriage was a second-class vocation, or that Catholics were not to give much attention to the Bible, gained widespread credence if not official sanction.

The Council of Trent contributed a great deal to the way the modern papacy took shape. Without feeling any need to justify such a perspective historically or theologically, it reaffirmed papal supremacy and submitted its decrees to the pope for approval. It also gave the pope the task of tying up loose ends that the council had not had time to resolve. Without explanation, the council gave the pope absolute, unrestricted power in the Church. In effect, Trent smashed a bottle of champagne on the bow of an autocratic papacy and cheered it down the slips and into the waters of modern history. This fact would have tremendous repercussions in the centuries to come.

In turn, bishops received absolute control over their dioceses, and by extension, pastors could exercise unquestioned authority in their parishes. This left the laity with a passive role in the Church, a situation understandable at the time and even necessary when most laity were illiterate. All the same, the Council of Trent ushered in the age of "pay, pray, and obey" for lay Catholics.

The Council of Trent put an end to some of the worst abuses in the Church's entire history, and it responded calmly, clearly, and with balanced statements to some of the Protestant Reformation's more out-of-kilter perspectives. It has even been said that if the Council of Trent's teaching on justification had been available to Luther, the Protestant Reformation would never have happened.

At the same time, Trent gave birth to a spirit in the Church that encouraged a privatized, implicitly antifamily spirituality, little contact with Scripture, liturgical individualism, and blind intolerance for religious differences, even on matters of secondary importance to an authentic Christian life.

In the present ecumenical era, of course, Catholics and Protestants are learning to view one another with a new sense of charity and tolerance, and there are the beginnings today of a new Catholic "turn to the family," which acknowledges the central place played by family in virtually everyone's life. Perhaps the differences that fueled the Reformation and the Council of Trent will one day be resolved so there can be a reunion to some form of Christian unity. And God willing, one day family life will play the vital role it is meant to play in Catholic spirituality.[9]

The ultramontanist movement, which in its most extreme form embraced bizarre attitudes toward the pope, was rooted in secular politics as well as in perceptions current in some circles that the Church was afflicted with doctrinal flabbiness. The ultimate thrust of the ultramontanes was toward not just a strong papacy, but a papacy that would possess absolute power and authority in the Church. One essential element of this kind of papacy would be universal infallibility.

CHAPTER 9

Ultramontanism and the First Vatican Council

Along with the Council of Trent, the First Vatican Council gave the Roman Catholic Church the shape it had until the early 1960s. Trent did its job well. If it can be charged with one serious oversight it would be its failure to respond to questions about the nature of the Church and the role of the papacy.

Trent turned over to the pope the implementation of the council's decrees with no provision for consultation with the other bishops. Only following Vatican II (1962–65) would a representative body of the world's bishops begin to meet as a synod in Rome every two years to deliberate on issues of ongoing concern to the whole Church and to advise the pope.

In effect, Trent handed the reins to the papacy and said, "Take us where you will." Following Trent, the pope appointed a committee of cardinals who shared his understanding of the Church to carry out implementation of the council's decrees, but he retained the authority to make final decisions. In addition to the constraints of events that prevented Trent from doing more, this bow to a narrow view of papal supremacy was also due to the council's lack of an adequate historical perspective on the Church.

Following the Council of Trent, therefore, the popes were for the most part ecclesiastical Lone Rangers. This had the advantage of getting things done in the way that any autocratic leadership can get things done, since there is little need to take the thoughts and concerns of others into account. But it had this major drawback: it limited the implementation of Trent's decrees to a single perspective, that of the pope.

In fact, the post-Tridentine popes did a good job up until the end of the sixteenth century, which amounts to about forty years. After that, the papacy reverted to many of its old ways. Luxury and elegant living returned to the

Vatican. The popes apparently believed that the best way to impress on the world the Church's conviction that the pope was truly the representative of Christ on earth was to bathe the papacy in wealth and comfort, such as a king might enjoy. The defense of the papal states — the pope's territorial holdings in Italy — seemed the primary task of the papacy, rather than to proclaim the Gospel and guide the Church.

Throughout the seventeenth and eighteenth centuries, the popes seemed all but lost in nostalgia for the glorious days of yore when, so they supposed, all of Europe pledged allegiance to them. Unfortunately, this sense of nostalgia and regular attempts to restore the papacy to its former grandeur, which had never really existed, blinded the popes to historical trends that led to world-class social upheavals such as the French Revolution (1793–94) and its Reign of Terror, during which thousands of people literally lost their heads to the guillotine. While the popes dreamed of yesterday, the foundations were shaking. This was not the papacy's finest hour.

In 1846 Pius IX — in Italian, *Pio Nono* — became pope. He was a profoundly religious man who opposed all that the Enlightenment stood for, including the use of reason and the pursuit of human dignity. For Pio Nono, the papacy and the Church were the last stronghold of truth in the face of social revolutions based on the desire for human rights.

Pius IX was not, to be sure, a two-dimensional man, and it would be unfair to portray him as such. He was only fifty-four when he became pope, and his pontificate was unusually long, thirty-two years (1846–78). Pius did not have a strong personality, but he found it easy to "win friends and influence people." He loved being with people, and his piety was sincere; indeed, many called him a saint during his lifetime. Many others, however, accused him of being little more than an egotistical autocrat. The distance that time provides offers some objectivity, as Church historians Roger Aubert et al. point out:

> In his youth [Pius IX] suffered from epileptic attacks which left him with an extreme excitability. It makes understandable many of his summary declarations and the fact that he frequently changed his mind according to the opinion last heard. Consequently, many observers regarded him as a hesitant and indecisive person. Only when he was convinced that it was a matter of consequence did he demonstrate unshakable resolution and boldly defended his position.[1]

Like most of the Italian priests of his generation, raised during a time that was unsettled in the world as well as in the Church, he did not receive a good education. "His superficial training often did not permit him to recognize the complexity of problems or the implications of many statements which he was expected to judge."[2]

Although he was good at applying common sense to issues, Pio Nono was also sometimes handicapped by curial advisers who were out of touch with reality.

Pius IX was a genuinely good, if impulsive, person. He did not have a strong intellect, but he had many interests, and in his youth he had read widely. As a young priest, he had no interest in advancing his career. Instead, he worked with orphans and the poor. He was a man of prayer, although he tended to attach too much importance to prophecies and purported miracles. He was also inclined to interpret world events as part of a great battle between God and Satan.

Pius was a classic "study in contrasts." As far as his pontificate is concerned, however, the bottom line seems to be that he was largely incapable of distinguishing between positive and negative developments either in the Church or in the world. For him, new was bad and a change of whatever kind was automatically undesirable.

The immediate predecessor of Pius IX was Gregory XVI, who had "rejected the separation of Church and state, denounced liberty of conscience as sheer madness and referred to liberty of the press as abominable and detestable."[3] So it is obvious that Pio Nono did not originate the attitudes toward the modern world that he embodied. A great fan of a rigidly conservative movement in the Church called ultramontanism, Pius IX saw this movement as the Church's only hope in the face of increasing secular indifference and government interference.[4] Ultramontanism would be at the very heart of the First Vatican Council. Aubert et al. explains:

> It is of great importance not to lose sight of the complex character of the ultramontane movement and its concrete reality. Its adherents propounded theological and canonical doctrines concerning the special privileges of the pope and the prerogatives of the Church over the civil power, developed a program for turning the ecclesiastical organization into a more authoritarian and centralistic one, favored restriction of the freedom of scholarship in philosophy and theology, and demanded a new outlook on piety which consisted less in an inner attitude than in frequent receipt of the sacraments and an increase in external devotions.[5]

The ultramontanist movement, which in its most extreme form embraced bizarre attitudes toward the pope, was rooted in secular politics as well as in perceptions current in some circles that the Church was afflicted with a kind of doctrinal flabbiness. The ultimate thrust of the ultramontanes was toward not just a strong papacy, but a papacy that would possess absolute power and authority in the Church. And one essential element of this kind of papacy would be universal infallibility.

Pio Nono supported the ultramontane movement because he believed it held the answers to the major crises in the society and Church of his time, and he saw it as the best response to "liberalism"—from the Latin *liber*, free—which he interpreted as a rejection of divine revelation. But also, in all humility, he believed himself to be infallible. This was by no means an original notion, of course. Pius IX didn't think up the idea one summer evening on a stroll around the Vatican gardens. Rather, it went back at least as far as Pope Gregory VII, who stated his belief in papal infallibility in 1073.

Pius apparently believed that the best way to firm up doctrinal beliefs, and the best way to strengthen the papacy and return it to its role as a highly respected authority in the world, would be to make papal infallibility an official doctrine of the Church. If the Protestant Reformation and the Enlightenment had seriously eroded the papacy's political and religious authority on the world stage, thought Pio Nono, to make papal infallibility a doctrine of the Church would show the world what was what. After all, no other leader could claim to be infallible.

If Pius IX could officially claim universal infallibility, this would enable him to battle rationalism, democracy, freedom of the press, and individual human rights; concepts he sincerely believed were destructive of civilization. The pope realized that the only way to accomplish such a doctrine would be to have it decreed by a Church council: How, then, to gather enough support to call a council that would proclaim such a doctrine?

Pius saw that the best way to convene a council would be to encourage ultramontanism and to make sure it was well represented when it finally met.

Ultramontanism was strongest in France and had many supporters in England and the United States. It was quite popular in Germany, too, but many members of the theological faculties in the universities opposed it.

Pio Nono took to appointing bishops only from among priests whose ultramontane credentials were in perfect order. The fact that he had been pope for twenty-four years when Vatican I convened in 1869 meant that he had, in effect, "stacked the deck" in his own favor. By this time there were 739 bishops in the world, and Pius IX had appointed all but 81 of them.

Ultramontanism embraced a form of scholastic theology that claimed Saint Thomas Aquinas as its source but that lacked Thomas's sophistication and rigorous intellectual honesty. Saint Thomas, for example, insisted that Christian theology should search out and celebrate truth wherever it might be found. For the ultramontanists, such an attitude smacked of heresy, for it would mean that the human mind might discover truth outside the pale of officially approved sources of divine revelation. Most of this ultramontanist neoscholastic theology was Saint Thomas watered down. There is no doubt, wrote John C. Dwyer, that "Rome was propagating neo-scholasticism not because of its theological depth or systematic brilliance, but because it offered a common denominator, on the basis of which seminary instruction could be standardized and unified throughout the Catholic world."[6] For ultramontanism tended to hold that the Church's universal nature demanded uniformity.

Riding the tidal wave of Marian devotion during these years, the French bishops began to appeal to the pope to proclaim the Immaculate

Conception of Mary as an official doctrine of the Church. On December 8, 1854, Pius IX stepped into a Vatican setting designed to communicate an aura of infallibility. The bishops in attendance were mere spectators along with everyone else as Pio Nono read the formal declaration that belief in the Immaculate Conception was from then on an essential part of Catholic faith and that anyone who denied this doctrine was a heretic.

As already noted, what made Pio Nono furious was liberalism—a term that summed up the spirit of the Enlightenment and belief in democracy, freedom of the press, and religious freedom. In the Church specifically, liberalism called for personal rights and no Church control over such matters as education and marriage.

In the 1850s Pius IX began to consider issuing a condemnation of all such "errors," and to this end he established a commission to study the question. There was, however, much opposition from bishops in countries with large Protestant populations, who thought that such a condemnation would needlessly make life difficult for Catholics in their countries.

Pius was not an unreasonable man, and he might have decided to skip the whole thing if two events had not occurred in 1863. In the first, a Belgian scholar, Count Montalembert, publicly defended a liberal Catholicism that, in embracing such ideals as freedom of the press and respect for human rights, was out of step with the kind of Catholicism the ultramontanes cherished.

The second event involved the German priest, John Joseph Ignaz von Döllinger, who publicly called on Rome to respect the right of theologians in German universities to freely pursue their academic research and discussions.

When Pius IX heard such talk, his anger intensified. This was precisely the kind of thinking that would be the downfall of Western civilization. So, on December 8, 1864, Pius issued an encyclical—a pastoral letter addressed to the whole Church—in which he drew up a list of what he regarded as the eighty most common "errors" of the day. This encyclical came to be called the *Syllabus of Errors*. It rejected such ideas as government control of public schools and separation of church and state, and ended with an outright condemnation of anyone who would champion absolute freedom of religion and freedom of the press. Pio Nono also condemned those who said that the papacy must leave the Middle Ages behind and adapt itself to the modern world.

In Protestant Europe, the crowd went wild with outrage. In Germany, the response was predictable, the ultramontanes sending up glad hosannahs, the liberals angry enough to chew nails. In England and the United States, ultra-montanes praised the *Syllabus,* liberal Catholics held their noses, and non-Catholics yawned and remarked that the whole business was silly.

The key reaction, however, came from Félix Dupanloup, the bishop of Orléans, France, who wrote an interpretation of the *Syllabus* that made the most ridiculous aspects of the document seem harmless, and clever man that he was, he did this in such a way that Pio Nono himself approved, more or less.

As a result of Bishop Dupanloup's interpretation of the *Syllabus,* liberal Catholic outrage in Europe soon subsided, except in Germany, where those who believed in academic freedom and freedom of the press continued to stew. The upshot of the whole affair was that the *Syllabus* made official the Church's "us versus them" mentality with regard to the modern world, and the door remained open for the continued growth of ultramontanism.

The ultramontane movement made steady progress, especially in France. Many French Catholics began to say that it was time to clothe the old idea of papal infallibility in the raiment of official Church doctrine. Pio Nono, for his part, lay low. But he thought papal infallibility a grand idea, since he had, in all humility, no doubt about being infallible, and not just in matters of faith, either. Recall that in

1854 he had, without so much as a blush, proclaimed the doctrine of the Immaculate Conception as binding on all Catholics. Pius had asked the bishops of the world for their views, but he alone made the decision with no mention of acting in union with the other bishops.

The ultramontane movement marched steadily on toward its goal, a formal declaration of the doctrine of papal infallibility. Anti-Protestant feeling among Catholics was at a high pitch, and in certain sections of the Church, especially France and Italy, ultramontanism slipped way over the line toward actual worship of the pope. After 1860, in fact, some historians suggest that a new form of ultramontanism developed, which should be called neo-ultramontanism.

During this period, some ultramontanes referred to the pope as a "Vice-God of Mankind" and as "Permanent Word Incarnate." From more than a few ultramontane pulpits came the startling message of "the three incarnations of the Son of God"—in the womb of the Blessed virgin, in the Eucharist, and in "the old man in the Vatican." One ultramontane periodical went so far as to insist that "when the Pope meditates, it is God who is thinking through him."[7]

Pio Nono planned Vatican I to be the final triumph of the Church over the evils of democracy, freedom of religion, freedom of speech, and freedom of the press. And to make sure everything went as planned, he appointed to the preparatory commission only men who supported ultramontanism.

Those who objected to what they saw as the abuses of ultramontanism were not about to lie down and play dead, however. There were many priests, bishops, and theologians who had serious difficulties with the whole idea. Unfazed by such spoilsports, however, the ultramontanists decided that the time was ripe to permanently rid the Church of all problems by calling a council to decree that the pope was infallible no matter what he said on any subject. "The Jesuit periodical *Civiltà Cattolica*," wrote John C. Dwyer, ". . . suggested that what all real Catholics wanted was a short council which would affirm the truth of the *Syllabus of Errors* and would then proclaim papal infallibility by acclamation (!)."[8]

One of the objections voiced by those who opposed ultramontanism was that the over-centralization of power in the papacy was unhealthy for the Church as a whole. They insisted that the office of bishop, as successor to the apostles, had divine origins and that to deny the bishops their proper role was to chip away at the basic structure of the Church. These critics of ultramontanism also believed that Pius IX wanted to require people to reject the entire modern world as a condition for remaining Catholic. They were convinced that there was virtually no historical or scriptural basis for a doctrine of papal infallibility. Pio Nono firmly believed, however, that his was the path of truth and the only answer to the evils of the modern world.

On June 26, 1867, Pius IX publicly announced that there would be a council. Two and a half years later, on December 8, 1869, he convened the First Vatican Council with seven hundred bishops in attendance. Pius, however, was an old man by now, and there is some historical uncertainty about his mental stability when the council opened. "The truth is that Pius IX, who was seventy-eight when Vatican I began, was often an embarrassment and was regarded by some of the Fathers of Vatican I as gaga."[9]

There were 60 prelates of Eastern Rite Churches, 200 bishops from outside Europe— 121 from North and South America, 49 of these from the United States—41 from India and the Far East, 18 from Oceania, and 9 Europeans from missions in Africa. Although this seems like a remarkably cosmopolitan group, more than one-third of the bishops were Italians, and combined with the French this group constituted an absolute majority.[10]

Although Vatican I discussed other topics, most notably the Church's missionary activities, the only significant action it took was on papal infallibility. The ultramontanes were led by Cardinal Manning, an English convert, and by the superior general of the Jesuits, whose name was Beckx. These bishops believed that to define papal infallibility would be to simply put the official stamp of approval on an aspect of Catholic belief that had been there from the beginning and was rooted in Scripture. They thought that what the world needed was more authority at a time when civilization was being undermined by democracy, which they viewed as a barely controlled form of anarchy.

"Rather than wrestle with the knotty problems raised by historical and biblical research," said Thomas Bokenkotter, "they preferred the easier recourse to an instant authority and systematically denounced to Rome all those who did not share their narrow theological views."[11]

The ultramontanes knew little about the history of the early Church, and they seemed to identify the traditions of scholastic theology and canon law with Sacred Tradition. Their perspective went back no further than the papacy of Gregory VII in the late eleventh century.

Only about one-third of the bishops at Vatican I opposed a formal definition of papal infallibility. These bishops did not, however, question the primacy of the pope as the head bishop of the Church. Rather, they believed that the pope could only make decisions binding on the whole Church when he acted in agreement with the other bishops.

Remarkably, the leader of the opposition seems to have been not a bishop but an English layman, Lord Acton, who, as a layman, was not allowed to attend the council. (How things had changed from the time of the earliest Church councils!) Lord Acton was, however, effective at bringing together opponents of ultramontanism and papal infallibility so they could have some impact on the council, in spite of their small numbers.

Even though it was uppermost in his mind, Pio Nono apparently thought it would be gauche to put the issue of papal infallibility on the council's agenda himself, so it didn't appear when the council opened. The ultramontane bishops took care of that little "oversight" in short order, though. With the pope's enthusiastic approval, they got papal infallibility on the agenda by circulating a petition that almost two-thirds of the bishops signed.

On May 13, 1870, after the successful circulation of another petition to move the discussion of papal infallibility forward on the agenda, the council turned to the issue that was on everyone's mind. The discussion was lengthy, but the opposition had the freedom to state its case fully. Thus, some balance began to enter the conversation. Eventually, most of the ultramontane bishops saw that their position needed to be qualified—there should be some limitations on papal infallibility.

Opponents of ultramontanism, on the other hand, began to realize that this idea of divine guidance for papal teachings, at least in some situations, was not without support in Sacred Tradition. Still, the argument continued with no end in sight, and the fact that the council was being held in a hall with bad acoustics was no help at all.

A critical moment came on June 18, 1870, when Cardinal Guidi, the superior general of the Dominican Order, offered a compromise. He stood up and suggested that the debate should shift from the infallibility of the pope to the infallibility of his doctrinal decisions.

"In Guidi's view," said Dwyer, "these decisions were infallible, precisely because they were made by the Pope *in concert with the other bishops;* the Pope could only teach infallibly when he acted in union with his fellow bishops and when he respected the tradition of the Church."[12]

When Pius heard Cardinal Guidi's words, he almost came unhinged. "Tradition!" he said. "I *am* Tradition!"[13]

All the same, perhaps due to an awareness that the pope's mental stability could no longer be relied upon, the council shifted its perspective to one that dealt with the doctrinal decisions of the pope, rather than with the pope himself, which made the extreme ultramontanists deeply unhappy and Pio Nono furious. As the time drew near for a vote, about eighty bishops were still opposed to a decree on infallibility as worded, so they packed their bags and left Rome rather than fuel the pope's anger any further.

On July 18, while a tremendous storm of lightning and thunder raged outside, a majority of the bishops present voted in favor of the "Constitution on the Infallible Teaching Authority of the Roman Pontiff." The final count was 533 for, 2 against. One of the two dissenting bishops was from the United States.[14] The central statement of this constitution said that the pope teaches infallibly when he teaches *ex cathedra* ("from the papal throne") on a matter of faith or morals.

This is a very carefully worded doctrine that makes a subtle but important distinction between the pope himself and what the pope teaches under certain conditions. What Vatican I taught was that under certain strictly limited circumstances the pope teaches infallibly, not that he himself is an infallible person.

The nuances of this doctrine have often failed to make it intact into the world at large. Many non-Catholics, and more than a few Catholics, believe that the pope himself is infallible. It is not uncommon for non-Catholics to think that for Catholics the pope is infallible no matter what he says or when. This "aura of infallibility" around the papacy was clearly not intended by Vatican I.

Before the council could continue, the Franco-Prussian War broke out, which, in effect, brought Vatican I to an end. A month later, Pius officially declared the council adjourned indefinitely. He was bitterly disappointed with the final decree on infallibility.

Pius IX accomplished much good for the Church during his pontificate, especially with regard to the deepening of the Church's piety and spirituality. He guided many of the old religious orders toward genuine renewal, and many new religious orders and congregations were founded during his tenure on the throne of Peter.

It is also important to point out that ultramontanism had its good effects. The piety promoted by ultramontanism encouraged frequent reception of the sacraments, devotion to Mary, and other devotions, some of which, it's true, went too far in the direction of sentimental devotionalism. Although it was guilty of more than a few excesses, ultramontanism still deserves credit for an authentic contribution to the renewal of Catholic spirituality by its emphasis on the central place of Christ in Catholic life.

The final word, however, must be this: The Vatican I doctrine on infallibility, though invoked only twice since it was decreed in 1870, in both cases with regard to Marian doctrines, generated almost constant theological controversy and has been a major problem in ecumenical discussions. It also started a drift in the direction of viewing the papacy as an end in itself rather than in the service of the Church and the Gospel. This drift would have more than a little to do with the modernist crisis of the nineteenth century, to which the next chapter will turn.

Fundamentally, the modernist crisis was an extremely unpleasant encounter between the modern scientific and historical frame of mind and a papacy that believed that nothing good happened after the thirteenth century. Typically, there was truth and error on both sides of the debate, but some seventy years later it is almost impossible to view the whole affair as little more than a massive failure on the part of Church authorities to provide the kind of leadership Catholics most needed at the time.

CHAPTER 10

Pius X and the Modernist Crisis

The Enlightenment of the 1700s gave birth in the following century to a new perspective that reshaped the Western mind. Central to this new worldview was the conviction that the sciences coupled with historical studies could result in discoveries and insights that would help to improve the quality of human existence. This new mindset spawned the technological society, which in turn led to such wonders as the automobile, the nuclear bomb, antibiotics, acid rain, television and videocassette recorders, smog, jet air travel, biological and chemical weapons, personal computers, the Nazi death camps of

World War II, shopping malls, plastics, and ready-to-eat frozen waffles—in short, the modern way of life.

Perhaps it was inevitable that such a perspective would, in the early twentieth century, frighten the bejeepers out of some people. This was especially true of Church authorities, who intuitively sensed that there was more to this new scientific and historical point of view than met the eye. At any rate, the new worldview with its dependence on science and history collided with the official Catholic viewpoint, which restricted the sources of truth to divine revelation, including the teachings of the Church.

As scientific and historical studies progressed, some Catholic scholars spied opportunities to give the traditional faith a new expression, which would do justice to the new worldview. As usual in such situations, people tended to gravitate either right or left. Some Catholics perceived the opportunity to apply scientific and historical methods to theology as the dawn of a new era. Others—particularly the pope and his advisers—interpreted this new mindset as the advent of a gargantuan disaster.

Church leaders in the early 1900s who objected to the application of the scientific and historical methods to the life of the Church called those open to the new ideas *modernists*. In fact, it is not easy to explain what *modernism* was all about. One group of Church historians defines it as "the meeting and confrontation of a long religious past with a present which found the vital sources of its inspiration in anything but this past."[1]

Others suggest that although the various modernist trends had unique interests and perspectives, they had in common "an undue confidence in contemporary developments and a rejection of that unconditional obedience which the Roman authorities had come to expect."[2]

Fundamentally, the modernist crisis was an extremely unpleasant encounter between the modern scientific and historical frame of mind and a papacy which believed that nothing good happened after the thirteenth century. Typically, there was truth and error on both sides of the debate, but some seventy years later it is almost impossible to view the whole affair as little more than a massive failure on the part of Church authorities to provide the kind of leadership Catholics most needed at the time. It was, in the view of many Church historians, "a catastrophe for the Church."[3]

The antimodernism of the papacy during this period was, however, not just a matter of shortsightedness or narrowmindedness. For the Church as a whole was deeply unsettled by questions raised by scholars who employed the new scientific and historical methods. Charles

Darwin, for example, brought into question the traditional interpretation of biblical teachings on the origins of the human race, and Sigmund Freud challenged the existence of God and of the human soul. So there was legitimate cause for concern.[4]

Ah well, said the modernists, there is no need to fear the historical and scientific methods in themselves. Perhaps we can even use these methods to explain and interpret the Christian faith in ways that will make it more acceptable and beneficial to the twentieth-century mind and heart.

Fifty years later, at the Second Vatican Council, the Church's leaders would agree, but their counterparts in the early 1900s were too blinded by fear of the unknown to have patience with such talk. To be fair, who could have guessed at the time that "the outcome of this renewed questioning, induced by a collective change of mind, would not necessarily lead to a total elimination of the essence of the Christian faith"?[5]

There are clear spiritual and psychological connections between antimodernism and the ultramontane movement of the mid-1800s. However, the roots of antimodernism, per se, can be traced most directly to the pontificate of Leo XIII (1878–1903).

In an encyclical issued in August 1879, Pope Leo XII insisted that the philosophy of the thirteenth-century scholar and saint Thomas Aquinas was, apart from divine inspiration, the best way to nail down philosophical truth. Leo believed that what the world needed was a return to the reverence the Middle Ages had held for Christian philosophy. He scorned the suggestion that because the world had changed a great deal since the Middle Ages, the Church's perspectives must adapt accordingly.

The attempt by Leo XIII to all but canonize the writings of Saint Thomas ran counter to the mood in certain Catholic academic circles, a mood that was open to scientific and historical methods of research and analysis. Leo's response was to urge theologians to confine Catholic theology to commentary on classical theological texts, primarily those of Aquinas, and to metaphysical speculation.

Some Catholic theologians, who forged ahead with the new methods of study, showed that over the centuries the Church had frequently changed its manner of presenting its teachings. This made Leo XIII and his supporters—to borrow a phrase from the early nineteenth-century Danish philosopher Søren Kierkegaard—"as nervous as a sparrow in a dance of cranes," because it suggested that change was possible now. For Leo, the philosophy of Aquinas was the only acceptable way to present Catholicism.

Thus originated the notion that later in the century became so widespread in the Church, the idea that Catholic theology should be dedicated exclusively to the reading and interpretation of the writings of Saint Thomas Aquinas and a few other classical authors.

In 1893, after some Catholic historians and theologians began to express an interest in the historical development of the Church and its doctrines, Pope Leo XIII issued another encyclical. This time he gave cautious approval to historical research for biblical studies, but he said that too much reliance on such methods could be dangerous.

To illustrate what he meant, Leo said that any errors or contradictions in the Bible are merely the result of mistakes made by those who copied the now lost original manuscripts. This implied that in the original documents divine inspiration would not have allowed for any such errors or contradictions, whether they related to matters of faith or not.

After Leo XIII died in 1903, Cardinal Giuseppe Melchior Sarto was elected pope and took the name Pius X. This name was appropriate, since the previous Pius, "Pio Nono," had been the one to spearhead the Vatican's ultramontane battle with the modern world in the mid-nineteenth century, a battle that Sarto as Pius X would take up again in all good faith.

As a young priest, Giuseppe Sarto engaged in pastoral work and became the chancellor of his diocese, Treviso, from 1875 to 1884. He then became bishop of Treviso and, in 1892, a cardinal and patriarch of Venice. His election to the papacy on August 4, 1903, would not have happened had not Austria vetoed the nomination of another cardinal who was the favorite candidate.

Pius X deserves credit for beginning the codification of canon law, for setting up a commission to revise the Latin (Vulgate) version of the Bible, for reorganizing the papal court, and for ordering a revision of the breviary, the official Latin prayer book then used by priests. He also countered inappropriate feelings of "unworthiness" among Catholics about receiving Holy Communion. Instead, he encouraged the frequent reception of Communion, especially by children. In this sense, Pius X had a profound effect on the spiritual renewal of the Church.

Pope Pius XII, who published an encyclical that was the last gasp of antimodernism, canonized Pius X a saint in 1954, the first pope to be so honored since Pius V, in 1712. Many a Catholic schoolchild of the mid-1950s received from a teaching nun a holy card or First Communion certificate decorated with a rosy, romanticized portrait of the new saint.

A major thrust of the papacy of Pius X was, however, his personal crusade against modernism. Unfortunately, in this he was handicapped by a medieval perspective on Catholic orthodoxy that was "nothing less than a scandal,"[6] a perspective that postponed for more than half a century the reestablishment of cordial relations between the Church's thought and that of the modern world. This is an excellent illustration of the fact that being canonized a saint does not mean that the holy one had no faults or blind spots. The truth is that the modernist crisis might never have happened had not Pius X felt obliged to "meddle in areas in which he was totally incompetent."[7]

During the nineteenth century, historical studies by theologians made much progress in showing how doctrine developed over the centuries. This was especially true in the German universities where both Protestant and Catholic theologians made great strides. John C. Dwyer comments:

> These studies made it clear that there was much in the doctrine and dogma of the Christian churches which had not existed from the beginning, but which had assumed its present form as a result of slow evolution over the years. These studies also made it

clear that scripture was totally misunderstood if it was read as a naively literal account of events which were historical in the modern sense of the word.[8]

This new historical approach to theological studies attracted much favorable attention toward the end of the 1800s, even outside Germany. At the same time, however, these new ideas were on a collision course with official interpretations of Saint Thomas Aquinas's writings, which insisted that certain formulations of religious truth transcended history and were thus not subject to new forms of expression. The idea that, in order to remain faithful to Scripture and Sacred Tradition, an eternal truth might require different formulations for different times and cultures was completely abhorrent to the antimodernist Roman perspective.

One of the most prominent figures in the modernist crisis was a French priest with a keen intellect and a great talent for writing, Alfred Loisy (1857–1940). Loisy used the new historical methods to study both Scripture and the Church.

In 1902 Father Loisy published *The Gospel and the Church,* in which he suggested that the Gospels are not meant to be a historical account of Jesus' life and ministry. Rather, he contended, the Gospels are records of the early

Church's faith experience. "Jesus announced the coming of the kingdom of God," wrote Loisy, "and what transpired was the Church."[9]

In 1964 the Pontifical Biblical Commission would virtually give a stamp of approval to the main thrust of Loisy's thought, but in 1903 there was no way the Vatican was about to tolerate what seemed to be pure and simple heresy.[10]

Loisy said that "while neither the institutional Church nor the sacraments are spelled out in detail in the Bible, Jesus' rudimentary teaching evolved, under the inspiration of the Holy Spirit, into the . . . second-century Church, and from there to the Church we know today."[11]

What Alfred Loisy did for the first time was to argue for the superiority of Catholicism to Protestantism strictly on the basis of scientific-historical studies. And what Leo XIII did was gasp and condemn him for it because be didn't arrive at his conclusions by the officially approved methods. The Vatican took no notice of the fact that most modernist writing was done to refute liberal Protestant opinions, not to change the Church's dogmas.

Two months after *The Gospel and the Church* appeared, the archbishop of Paris denounced it, and seven months later, after Pius X was elected, the antimodernist pot began to boil in earnest.

Loisy wrote a second book, wherein he said that Jesus' birth from a virgin, his resurrection, and his divine nature, cannot be scientifically proven—an idea that today draws little more than a yawn because few Catholics and other mainstream, nonfundamentalist Christians feel any need to justify faith scientifically. Instead, wrote Loisy, the Church's formal doctrines on these points are "evidence of what the Church came to believe about Jesus."[12]

In about two shakes, on December 16, 1903, Rome lowered the boom. Pius X condemned Loisy's writings in no uncertain terms, and the Frenchman submitted, for the time being, to an order of silence.

Loisy later said that he had lost faith in Christ and in a personal God before he wrote his two books, but that he had hoped to hide this fact and remain in the Church to reform it from the inside because he believed it had humanitarian value, which just goes to show that on a technical level it doesn't take faith to do theology. Loisy died peacefully in 1940, without ever seeking formal reconciliation with the Church.

The final word on Loisy seems to be that he had many positive and legitimate ideas, but he did not think them through far enough. He caused much anxiety in the Church, especially among a clergy educated in a Council of Trent-inspired seminary system that ill prepared them to face either the twentieth century or the questions the modernists raised.

In spite of the uproar over Loisy, the kinds of ideas he discussed and the methods he used would not go away. Other sincere, faith-filled Catholic scholars adopted the scientific-historical methods to write everything from biographies of saints to philosophy, and from systematic theology to biblical studies. Of course, Pius X denounced them all.

Still, modernism was hard to define. It was not a well-organized theological system. The English modernist George Tyrrell (1861–1909) wrote that a modernist was "any Christian of any denomination who is convinced that the essential truths of his religion and the essential truths of modern society can enter into a synthesis."[13]

Tyrrell also said that revelation is not a series of verbal formulae, but primarily an experience of the divine. He wanted a democratic Church, and thought the antimodernist methods of Pius X were a tremendous abuse of authority in the Church. Pius excommunicated Tyrrell in 1907, and he died soon thereafter. Like Loisy, Tyrrell died without being formally reconciled with the Church, but he proclaimed his love for the Church to the end nevertheless.

Anthony E. Gilles offers a good description of modernism's central ideas:

> Those accused of being Modernists differed widely in their views, but they all

tended to support the following ideas: (1) adherence to a historical-critical method in biblical research which did not attempt to deny contradictions and inconsistencies; (2) a preference for a theology of action and involvement as opposed to a speculative, "ivory-tower" theology which never entered into contact with the real world; and (3) a belief in the evolution of doctrine toward an ever fuller appreciation of the Church's mission, as opposed to the traditionalists' attempt to fix normative doctrine in a past era of greatness, such as the 13th century.[14]

Antimodernists accused modernists of denying that the Bible was inspired by God and of rejecting the proposition that the philosophy of Saint Thomas Aquinas was superior to all other philosophical systems. They also charged modernists with denying that Church authorities have supremacy over the opinions of theologians.

In July 1907 the Vatican let the modernists have it with both barrels. The Holy Office, successor to the Office of the Holy Inquisition, which was in charge of spotting heresies, published a decree, sometimes called the "New Syllabus of Errors," which condemned sixty-five modernist tendencies and outlined various ways to keep modernism out of seminaries and schools.

In the same month, Pius X issued an encyclical in which he attempted to impose a systematic structure on modernism. He accused modernism of, among other things, "immanentism," which asserts that human religious experience begins not with an experience of the divine but with consciousness of an inner religious need. This, Pius said, leads to agnosticism and evolutionism, which he defined as meaning that everything in the Church is subject to *substantial* change.

Most modernist scholars, when they read the Holy Office's decree and the pope's encyclical, blinked in disbelief. For none of them had ever said what these two documents accused them of saying. Then, in November 1907, the Holy Office announced that anyone who disagreed with the pope's encyclical would be excommunicated.

Thomas Bokenkotter comments on the antimodernist encyclical of Pius X:

> It presumes bad faith and imputes evil motives to zealous Catholic scholars who were at least asking the right questions, and it presents a sad spectacle of the highest authority in the Church resorting to sarcasm and invective in what was supposed to be a magisterial judgment; it abounds in

such harsh phrases as "poisonous doctrines . . . most pernicious of all the adversaries of the Church . . . the root of their folly and error . . . boundless effrontery. . . ."

To extirpate Modernism, the Pope called for measures that smacked of the worst features of the medieval Inquisition.[15]

Pius X ordered every diocese to set up a "vigilance committee," and to name censors, to spot and denounce any sign of modernism that might crop up. And these groups were to do all their work in complete secrecy.

On June 29, 1908, the Vatican minted a coin to celebrate the fifth anniversary of the pontificate of Pius X. On the coin the pope was pictured slaying the modernist dragon. Some modernist scholars, with much hoopla, left the Church of their own accord or were excommunicated. Most, however, submitted obediently to Rome and gave up their modernist scholarship.

It was perhaps necessary for the Vatican to react in such a negative fashion to modernism in order to point out those aspects of modern thought that clashed with official Church teachings. Perhaps, too, the first responsibility of the pope was to protect the faith of millions of uneducated, unsophisticated Catholics who might have been deeply disturbed had the ideas of the modernists circulated widely. Undoubtedly, too, modernist scholars were sometimes too cavalier with their opinions and let themselves be carried away by enthusiasm when they should have tempered their writings with a dash more of intellectual humility.

Be all this as it may, the way Pius X dealt with modernism resulted in the virtual suppression of creative Catholic scholarship for many years to come. "Catholic seminaries," wrote Bokenkotter, "remained medieval ghettos until the middle of the twentieth century, and future priests were taught a biblical fundamentalism embroidered with theories like the one that proved Jonah could have lived inside the whale since a French scholar had found toads that lived inside stones for thousands of years."[16]

Perhaps it would have been better for the Church over the long haul if Pius X had looked for what might be of value in modernist thought and would have been less anxious to find a modernist around every corner.

In an attempt to make sure that modernism did not raise its ugly head again, in 1910 Pius X required that all seminary professors, teachers of theology, priests, and candidates for the priesthood annually take an antimodernist oath.

For Pius X, modernism was "the M word," and he continued to fear it until the end of his life. He once confided that he felt modernism was far worse than what Martin Luther had started. Thus, the fears of Pius gave birth to a well-orchestrated effort to squelch even the slightest tendency to wander from the officially approved path.

In the years following the 1907 decree of the Holy Office and the antimodernist encyclical of Pius X, militant supporters called themselves "integral Catholics." As one such enthusiast wrote, ". . . we prefer over everything and everybody not only the traditional doctrine of the Church in regard to absolute truths, but also the directives of the Pope in the area of pragmatic contingencies. The Pope and the Church are one."[17]

Thus, hand in glove with the official denunciations of modernism by Church authorities went a barrage of "integralist" condemnations that became more and more common as the pontificate of Pius X wore on. A. Carollanti, an active early antimodernist, wrote:

> Arianism, Pelagianism, and Jansenism [Christian heresies all], having appeared after their condemnation by the Church, left a trail of errors that became known as semi-Arianism, semi-Pelagianism, and semi-Jansenism. Likewise, today, modernism, fatally exposed, has left after its departure other kinds of errors, sprouting all over like seeds and threatening to ruin, or ruining,

many a good Catholic. . . . I repeat, there is a semimodernism that, although not as ugly as its antecedent, is much more deceptive and insidious, a modernism that proposes to be a synthesis of all heresies.[18]

No one was safe from the integralists' Inquisition-like strategies. With more than a few similarities to the rabid anticommunism of the mid-1950s McCarthy era in the United States, those behind integralism were irresponsible censors who were theologically incompetent and especially unqualified to critique biblical scholarship. A fearful Vatican forbade Catholic scholars from discussing whether Moses himself wrote the first five books of the Old Testament, whether Isaiah had more than one author, whether Matthew was the first Gospel written, and whether Paul wrote the Letter to the Hebrews.[19]

It's not as if antimodernism had no critics in high places. Certain Church leaders did recognize that the tactics of the integralists were ridiculous, such as the Italian Cardinal Andrea Ferrari, who wrote: "It is sad that some are obliged, even publicly, to act excessively, detecting modernism almost everywhere and denouncing it, and that they even want to suspect men of modernism who are far from it."[20]

The integralists used denunciations, clandestine methods, and even espionage to pursue their ends. But they also worked out in the open by publishing books, brochures, and journals, albeit of small circulation. Pius X gave financial support to an Italian integralist journal.

Before it was all over there was a well-orchestrated, Vatican-directed, international, antimodernist secret organization, including a network of spies in important dioceses who kept their work under wraps and communicated by means of a secret code. This organization's efforts had pathetic results, however, even while it enjoyed the full support of the pope. Such a secret organization is one "which," commented Aubert et al., in an understatement of Wagnerian proportions, "does not seem permissible to us today. . . ."[21]

The "integral Catholics," zealous defenders of their understanding of orthodoxy, continued to beat the same old drum, charging "modernists" and "liberals" with watering down the Faith. They insisted that they themselves maintained "the true Faith," and nothing but — until, of course, a pope might come along who said something they disagreed with. It is not that the primary motive behind integralism was egotism. Rather, the "integral Catholics" saw themselves as fulfilling a mission from God.

In 1911 integralists denounced to Rome a young priest named Angelo Giuseppe Roncalli—the future Pope John XXIII—for an article he had written. Since Roncalli would play such a key role in the Church's "turn toward the modem world" at Vatican II, it may be of special interest to look, however briefly, at what the future pope was up to when the whirlwind of antimodernism was at its wildest.[22]

Four months after the 1907 antimodernist decree and Pius X's like-minded encyclical, Roncalli, a twenty-four-year-old professor of Church history at the seminary in Bergamo, delivered a lecture. Roncalli cheerfully stated that he believed it was important for the Church to face up to the issues raised by the modern world. He defended historical criticism, but explained that it was the Church itself, through the work in the 1600s of Cesare Baronius—Church historian, cardinal, and friend of Saint Philip Neri—that had opened the way to this kind of research some three hundred years earlier. This was a historical fact, the young priest said, which did much honor to the Church.

Roncalli as much as said that he thought the modernists had some legitimate points to make. No dummy, he then showed from history that a widely admired cardinal who was a Church historian originated the methods the modernists were using. Who could fault such an argument?

In 1910, however, at the height of the antimodernist panic, when everyone was suspect and a Church career could be ruined overnight by a letter to the right person, Roncalli wrote a strong negative judgment of modernism and voiced his approval of the means adopted by Pius X. He also took the antimodernist oath required by the pope.

As the reign of integralism neared its end, in June 1914, Roncalli was flat-out accused by a cardinal of being a modernist. He responded by writing what his biographer calls a "grovelling" letter of denial, one that is impossible to reconcile with his lecture seven years earlier.[23]

In the end, when the worst of the antimodernist debacle was over, the future pope was much the wiser. "From the whole tragic episode Roncalli drew the conclusion that there were other and better ways of dealing with 'error' in the Church."[24]

Fortunately, the antimodernist witch hunt lasted only until the death of Pius X, in 1914, although its repercussions continued to have a chilling effect on the life of the Church well into the 1930s. Only Vatican II (1962–65) would finally put this particular ghost to rest with an unparalleled openness to the twentieth century.

One must add, however, that thus far indignant right-wing campaigns to save the Church from "errors" seem to be a small but noisy part of every phase of modern Church history. There always seem to be sincere Catholics who think that the only way to cope with the future is to retreat to the past. At the same time, one must acknowledge that a healthy Church will always make room for a blend of the old and the new.

In September 1914, Pope Benedict XV, successor to Pius X, found on his desk an unopened letter addressed to his predecessor. Benedict read the letter with astonishment, for it was a denunciation of himself as a modernist from an antimodernist Italian bishop.

The Church as a whole breathed an almost audible sigh of relief when Benedict XV began to restore a much-needed sense of balance to the Vatican. He dismissed papal advisers who were integralists and condemned integralism in his first encyclical. Benedict showed that the Church was not permanently committed to a reactionary response to the modern world and was, in fact, prepared to adopt a more positive outlook.

It is unfortunate that the Church entered the twentieth century on a frantic note of suspicion and fear. Well might Pius X have soberly considered some words of John Henry Newman, the great English convert, priest, theologian, and cardinal, who died a mere thirteen years before Pius became pope: "Nay, one cause of corruption in religion is the refusal to follow the course of doctrine as it moves on, and an obstinacy in the notions of the past."[25]

The Second Vatican Council opened on October 11, 1962, with little awareness of the revolutionary changes it would bring about in the life of the Church. . . . Many thought that the council would be little more than a ceremonial show. In his opening address, however, Pope John [XXIII] put to rest any such assumption. He delivered the deathblow to the antimodernist spirit of the last few popes and made it abundantly clear that he wanted the council to bring new life to the Church.

John XXIII
and the
Second
Vatican
Council

The pontificate of Pope John XXIII (1958–63) and the Second Vatican Council (1962–65) constitute what will probably be the most important religious event of the twentieth century. Pope John showed the world that a pope deeply rooted in Catholic tradition could be a warm, open-minded, humane person and a sign of love, compassion, and reconciliation. Vatican II showed that the oldest institution in the Western world had plenty of life in it yet.

Angelo Giuseppe Roncalli, the son of peasant farmers, was born November 25, 1881, in Sotto il Monte, in the province of Bergamo, Italy. He was the fourth of fourteen children and attended the minor and major seminaries in Bergamo from 1892 to 1900. He completed his theological studies at the Roman Seminary of Sant' Apollinare from 1901 to 1905, interrupted by one year of obligatory military service, which he disliked intensely. Roncalli received the doctorate in theology on July 13, 1904, and was ordained a priest on August 10, 1904.

Following his ordination, the young priest made a pilgrimage to the Holy Land, then became secretary to Giacomo Maria Radini Tedeschi, the new bishop of his home diocese of Bergamo. Beginning in October 1906, Roncalli also became a professor of Church history at the major seminary, where he lectured on the writings of the early fathers of the Church and apologetics as well as edited a theological journal.

The future pope would retain a lifelong interest in Church history and the early fathers, and this gave him a historical perspective on the Church uncommon in that era. During World War I, Roncalli served as a military chaplain and afterward became chaplain and spiritual director for the seminarians who had served in the military during the war.

Roncalli returned in 1920 to Rome, where for four years he directed the Italian work of the Propagation of the Faith. The Roman Curia regarded Roncalli as a personable but not-too-bright country bumpkin, so he was made a bishop in 1925 and spent ten years as papal representative in Bulgaria and another ten years in Turkey and Greece.

After World War II, however, since he was known to be an effective peacemaker in hostile situations, Pope Pius XII sent Archbishop Roncalli to France to deal with General Charles DeGaulle, who wanted to eject all bishops who had not opposed the puppet government set up during the war by the Nazis. Roncalli smoothed ruffled feathers with his usual good humor, grace, and practical grasp of politics.

Pius XII, who liked Roncalli, made him a cardinal on January 12, 1953, and three days later named him the new patriarch of Venice, a city whose people he grew to love.

From his days in the seminary to the end of his life, Angelo Roncalli was a thoroughly traditional Catholic in his piety. He read *The Imitation of Christ* and made the Spiritual Exercises of Saint Ignatius regularly. He also prayed the rosary daily, as well as his breviary—now called the Liturgy of the Hours—and went to confession weekly.

"The craftiness of the peasant," wrote Church historian Hubert Jedin, "was in [Roncalli] united to the humor of the peasant; of no pope since Benedict XIV have so many anecdotes been handed down."[1]

Roncalli lived in Rome for several years while studying theology, and he was in the service of the Roman Curia for almost thirty years. Yet he was no curialist, and he expressed frustration with the curia on more than one occasion. He paid more attention to the Gospels than to Vatican politics, although he was always obedient. He said that he simply wanted to be a good shepherd.

Before his departure for the October 1958 conclave—gathering of cardinals to elect a new pope—that would place him on the chair of Peter, Cardinal Roncalli confided to friends that he thought he might be elected pope. He showed the depth of his understanding of the historical aspect of the Church's nature when, before his departure, he told the seminarians of his diocese: "The Church is young; it remains, as constantly in its history, amenable to change."[2]

On October 28, 1958, at the age of seventy-six, Angelo Giuseppe Roncalli was elected pope. He took the name John XXIII. The members of the curia thought that the old man would make a good interim pope who would not rock the boat, but they were mistaken.

Two days later the new pope remarked for the first time that he thought the Church needed a council to reinvigorate it and bring it into the twentieth century. The members of the curia could not have been more shocked. In fact, some leading theologians of the time thought that Vatican I would be the last Church council. After all, once the pope is infallible what need is there for a council?

The world was charmed by Pope John, but not everyone was impressed. "He's no pope," muttered Cardinal Francis Spellman of New York, "he should be selling bananas."[3]

Within a few months, on January 22, 1959, the man the world would call "good Pope John" announced publicly for the first time that he would call a council. He invited all 2,594 of the world's bishops, plus the 156 major superiors of religious institutes, as well as members of Catholic university faculties of theology, to submit suggestions.

Few understood the value of what Pope John was doing. Even the man who would be the next pope, Archbishop Montini of Milan, said: "This holy old boy doesn't seem to realize what a hornet's nest he's stirring up."[4]

A mountain of "input" arrived in response to Pope John's invitation, and after it was sifted and analyzed, on June 5, 1960, the pope issued a document stating for the first time that the council would be called Vatican II. He then directed that ten preparatory commissions be formed. It would be the task of these commissions to write a first draft of the document on each of the various topics that the council would discuss. Because the preparatory commissions were all dominated by curial cardinals, however, the first drafts were almost all little more than summaries of papal statements from recent decades or mere summaries of status-quo theology. They did not embody the advances Pope John hoped for.

The Second Vatican Council opened on October 11, 1962, with little awareness of the revolutionary changes it would bring about in the life of the Church. Pope John had invited observers from Protestant and Eastern Orthodox Churches to attend, however, and this gave the council a truly ecumenical flavor. Some 2,540 council fathers presented themselves for this opening session, a number far greater than any earlier council. Remarkably, Catholic women, mostly nuns, were also invited but only as observers.

Pope John rode through the bronze doors of Saint Peter's Basilica in his *sedia gestatoria*, a chair carried on the shoulders of several strong men, but once inside he walked through the midst of the council fathers who were seated in banks of bleacher-like seats on both sides of the huge church. Pope John did not wear the traditional papal triple crown, a fact which had its intended effect. Instead, he wore the bishop's miter, a symbol of his desire that the papacy and the council have strong human and pastoral dimensions. As far as Pope John was concerned, triumphalism in the Church should go the way of the dinosaurs.

Many thought that the council would be little more than a ceremonial show. In his opening address, however, Pope John put to rest any such assumption. He delivered the final deathblow to the antimodernist spirit of the last few popes and made it abundantly clear that he wanted the council to bring new life to the Church. He said:

> In the everyday exercise of our pastoral ministry, greatly to our sorrow, we sometimes have to listen to those who although consumed with zeal do not have very much judgment or balance. To them the modern world is nothing but betrayal and ruination. They claim that this age is far worse than previous ages, and they go on as though they had learned nothing at all from history—and yet history is the great teacher of life. . . . We feel bound to disagree with

these prophets of misfortune who are forever forecasting calamity. . . .[5]

Pope John also said:

Today the Spouse of Christ [the Church] prefers to use the medicine of mercy rather than severity. She considers that she meets the needs of the present age by showing the validity of her teaching rather than condemnations.[6]

This pope, who was "free of all dogmatic narrowness and defensive anxiety,"[7] went on to make a distinction that would have a profound impact on the council. He declared that "authentic doctrine has to be studied and expounded in the light of the research methods and the language of modern thought. For the substance of the ancient deposit of faith is one thing, and the way in which it is presented is another."[8]

Pius IX must have been spinning in his grave. For conservatives at the council, who believed that the language of religious doctrine cannot change, this last remark was a sure recipe for a heart attack. It was "modernism" pure and simple. For progressives, on the other hand, who thought that all doctrinal formulations have a historical dimension, Pope John's words were like a breath of fresh air.

It wasn't long before John XXIII discovered that he could not rely on even the Vatican press to report his words accurately. When his opening address came out in the official collection of papal documents, the text had been tampered with to render it "safe." The section of his address quoted above now read: "For the . . . deposit of faith itself, or the truths which are contained in our venerable doctrine, is one thing, and the way in which they are expressed is another, retaining however the same sense and meaning."[9]

Which, of course, is theological smoke and mirrors.

Pope John shook his head in disbelief, then countered by quoting his real words at every opportunity in other talks he gave.

It would be a mistake to conclude that Pope John XXIII was an undisciplined liberal. Prior to the council, in fact, he made some perfectly conservative choices. He approved the decision to suppress the so-called worker-priests in France, appointed a conservative Cardinal Domenico Tardini as his Secretary of State, and insisted on the use of Latin in the liturgy and in theological studies.

As Vatican II began, the relationship of pope to council was weighted with much historical tension. As head of the council, the pope could intervene when difficulties arose.

He could approve decrees, but he could not refuse to approve them. Unlike some of his recent predecessors, however, John XXIII was not tied up in knots about the possibility that a council might move in directions he would not approve. Rather, Pope John quietly expected the Holy Spirit to work through the deliberations of the council. He felt that to attend all the council meetings might stifle honest discussion, so for the most part he worked in his office and observed the council proceedings from time to time on closed-circuit television.

Vatican II, gathered in the nave of Saint Peter's Basilica, was, for the first time in history, truly representative of the universal Church. It was also an autumn council, as all of its four sessions took place between the months of September and December.

Bishops were present from all five continents: 1,041 from Europe, 956 from North and South America, more than 300 from Asia, and 279 from Africa.[10]

The council received its distinctive character from a "tension-filled struggle between 'intransigent' and 'progressive' forces."[11] The "intransigent" group was numerically weaker but had a firm hold on the Roman Curia. The "progressives" were from central and western Europe, North America, and some mission countries.

In accordance with the wishes of the pope, it was decided in advance that the council would refrain from condemning "errors" in formal decrees. In this, Vatican II was different from all previous Church councils which felt perfectly justified in hurling condemnations in all directions where it seemed appropriate.

All the same, there is plenty of evidence to indicate that the curia planned to get control of the council right off the bat and not turn loose. They had, however, underestimated the spirit of the council.

The council fathers soon realized that they would have to seize control from the curia if the council was to accomplish anything like what Pope John had in mind. This meant that they would have to gain control of the ten twenty-four member commissions that would draw up and submit documents for the council to consider and vote on.

The curia had picked its own men, in advance, to chair these commissions and hoped to get them elected right away, but the first speaker at the council, Cardinal Achille Lienart, of Lille, France, put the kibosh on that particular curial fantasy. He stood up and asked how the bishops could be expected to vote for men they did not know. He then suggested that the bishops be allowed time to draw up their own lists of candidates to chair the commissions. The council agreed, and the curialists began to squirm, and well they might. Soon the council elected men to chair the commissions who were, for the most part, independents representing the various leanings of the world's bishops.

The next discovery the council fathers made was that most of the theological first draft papers that the curia had produced were worthless and needed to be completely rewritten. Only the document on the liturgy showed some promise; in fact, it was quite well done, reflecting a thorough awareness of the renewal in liturgical theology that had been going on for a long time before the council.

There were powerful voices on both sides, but it soon became clear that this would be a progressive council. "Archbishop Hallinan of Atlanta, Georgia," said Thomas Bokenkotter, "one of the champions of reform, noted how amusing it was at times to hear bishops speaking in elegant Ciceronian Latin while arguing for the use of the vernacular language [in the liturgy]."[12]

The first major rebellion took place on November 14, 1962, when the majority of the council fathers rejected the first draft of the document on divine revelation. Actually, the necessary two-thirds vote against the document failed by a few votes, but the mind of the council was clear enough that John XXIII ordered the document back to its commission for a rewrite.

On May 21, 1962, Pope John had written a memo in which he used strong language indeed:

> The time has come to put a stop to this nonsense. Either the Biblical Commission will bestir itself, do some proper work and by its suggestions to the Holy Father make a useful contribution to the needs of the present time, or it would be better to abolish it and let the Supreme Authority [i.e. the pope himself] replace it in the Lord by something else.[13]

The document on divine revelation was particularly important because it dealt with fundamental theological ideas. Therefore, the fact that the council gave the first, status-quo version such a resounding raspberry signaled a clear break with the theological traditions of the Council of Trent.

Still, the council had no firm sense of direction until Cardinal Léon-Joseph Suenens, of Belgium, rose to propose that the council focus on the Church, both in itself and in relation to the modern world. The council fathers approved with a huge outburst of applause, which violated council rules but it wouldn't be the last time.

The first session of Vatican II ended on December 8, 1962. No decrees had been approved, but the council fathers had showed the curia who was in charge and had enthusiastically embraced the ideals and spirit of Pope John XXIII.

At the closing ceremonies, the pope offered encouraging words. He told the bishops that agreement takes time and that he firmly believed that the Holy Spirit's will would be accomplished through the council.

New drafts of the documents that the council had rejected were sent out to the bishops in early May 1963 — and they were very different from the originals that the curially dominated commissions had produced.

Sadly, Pope John did not live to see the second session of the council begin the following September. He died on June 3, 1963, a victim of stomach cancer. "He had lived eighty-one and a half years," writes Peter Hebblethwaite, "been a priest for fifty-eight years, a bishop for thirty-eight years, and pope for less than five years — the shortest pontificate of the century so far. Yet in him the Church and the world were prodigiously blessed."[14]

John XXIII died, wrote Hubert Jedin, "mourned by the whole world, almost more outside than inside the Church."[15]

Pope John had dropped more than a few hints that he hoped his successor would be the archbishop of Milan, Giovanni Battista Montini, the first man he had made a cardinal. And thus it happened, on June 21, 1963. So widely expected was Montini's election that the newspapers reported that he was the new pope two hours before the official announcement.

Montini took the name Paul VI, and soon announced in a radio message that the council Pope John had called would continue. The new pope had the advantage of having participated in the council as an insider, so he "knew the opposition which had come out against the new course during the first session."[16]

Right away, however, Pope Paul VI put his own stamp on the council. He encouraged the bishops to invite more laity to serve as advisers and introduced the new category of "listeners," people invited to attend who would not be able to vote, including some women, mostly nuns.

On September 18, eleven days before the second session of the council opened, Pope Paul met with the members of the curia, telling them that he wanted no funny business from them this time around and that he expected their strict obedience.

When Pope Paul VI opened the second session of the council on September 29, 1963, he instructed the bishops to discuss a major document on the Church with special attention to its inner renewal, to the unity of all Christians, and to the Church's dialogue with the world.

More than a few mouths dropped open when Pope Paul said, with regard to the Church's relations with other Christian churches, that there was room for regret on both sides:

> If any guilt in the separation is ours, we humbly ask God's pardon and also seek forgiveness from the brethren who should have felt themselves separated from us; for our part, we are prepared to forgive the wrongs which have been done to the Catholic Church.[17]

The key debate during the second session was over the document on the Church, especially the section on the relationship between the pope and the bishops. The progressives, with ancient tradition on their side, argued for the right of the bishops as a group to share in the authority of the pope over the Church. For the conservatives, however, who found it tough to see any further back than the sixteenth-century Council of Trent, this was a terrible idea that undermined the monarchical style of papacy that had been embodied so well in Pope John's predecessor, Pius XII.

It soon became clear that politics was the name of the game, though certainly the Holy Spirit was at work, as Pope John had predicted. The solidly conservative commission responsible for the document on the Church led by the head of the Holy Office — in earlier times called the Office of the Holy Inquisition — Cardinal Ottaviani, dragged its feet heroically, employing every delaying tactic in the book. They were worried that the document as written detracted from the authority of the pope and would lead to chaos.

The four progressive moderators of the council, however, led by Cardinal Suenens, nearly executed an end run on the commission by proposing to submit five questions to the council that embodied the heart of the matter. This, they hoped, would reveal the mind of the council without having to wait on the commission. Cardinal Ottaviani called a foul, however, and a stormy battle of wits raged behind the scenes.

Finally, after Pope Paul drop-kicked a few well-placed hints, Ottaviani's commission agreed to let the questions be presented to the council, but just this once. As Cardinal Ottaviani and his commission feared, the vote revealed a solid majority in favor of the progressive viewpoint, which would downplay the old hierarchy-laity caste system in the Church and define the Church fundamentally as the People of God.

Parenthetically, just as it is a mistake to think of Pope John XXIII as a freewheeling liberal, it is just as much a mistake to think of Cardinal Ottaviani as having a closed mind. He was rigidly conservative, true, but he was also one of the first in the Vatican to declare nuclear weapons immoral.

After much debate, the Constitution on the Sacred Liturgy was approved on November 22, 1963, with special emphasis on the liturgy of the Word at Mass being in the vernacular only. This document stressed the need for full and active participation in the liturgy by the whole congregation. The reform of the various liturgical books, including the missal and the breviary, was left to a postconciliar commission.

Another dramatic moment occurred during this second session when Cardinal Frings of West Germany verbally boxed Cardinal Ottaviani's ears for the techniques the Holy Office used habitually with writers whose work it frowned upon. The usual approach was to condemn such writers without giving them a chance to defend themselves. Cardinal Ottaviani, "the old, nearly blind son of a baker from the tough Roman Trastevere slums," stood and responded that such a criticism could only come from ignorance.[18]

The third session began on November 14, 1964, with the first concelebration of the Mass.

Five other priests joined the pope at the altar. Central to this session was the debate on the much-improved document on revelation. This document now reflected an acceptance of the modern historical methods of biblical research and interpretation, in tune with the ground-breaking 1947 encyclical of Pope Pius XII, *Divino Afflante Spiritu.*

The document on the Church in the modern world also received much attention and ended up being the longest document issued by the council. This document called for the Church to engage in dialogue with the world, not close itself off.

At one point, three European cardinals urged reconsideration of the official Church prohibition of artificial methods of birth control, but Pope Paul removed the item from the agenda, saying that he would have it studied by a special commission after the council.[19]

A dramatic moment came when, contrary to the wishes of the majority, the document on religious liberty—which said that no one had the right to coerce anyone else on matters of religion—was shelved through the efforts of the conservative minority, represented by a curial cardinal, Eugene Tisserant. The announcement came that there would be no vote on this document at this session of the council. Bokenkotter describes the scene:

The words brought the bishops to their feet; they swarmed into the aisles and milled around, obviously dismayed and upset. Someone grabbed a piece of paper, and a petition was hastily drawn up on the spot, quickly signed by more than four hundred, and then presented immediately to the pope. . . . Paul refused, however, to contravene Tisserant's decision, and the matter was left hanging in suspense until the fourth session.[20]

As the third session drew to a close, many bishops were irritated by several papal interventions to pacify the conservative minority. One change made by the pope emphasized papal primacy and weakened the notion of the pope's unity with the other bishops. Another made the document on ecumenism less open to Protestant churches. To compound the progressive bishops' irritation, Pope Paul slipped these changes in at the last minute so the bishops felt they had to vote in favor or lose the whole document.

The fourth and final session of Vatican II opened on September 14, 1965. Pope Paul surprised everyone by announcing that he would organize a Synod of Bishops to help him to work for the welfare of the Church.

The council fathers knew that this was to be the last session, so they were under pressure to get much work done. The first item on the agenda was the delayed vote on the document on religious liberty. The conservative minority was having fits about the document's declaration that no one has the right to force or contradict a person's conscience on matters of religious belief, and the admission that the Church had not always respected this principle. All to no avail, however. Pope Paul intervened to call for an immediate vote on the document as it stood, and it was approved by an overwhelming majority.

The fourth session also approved documents on the pastoral office of bishops, on the renewal of religious life, and on the formation of priests. The latter document made the important observation that the family is "a sort of first seminary" for vocations to the priesthood, an insight that carries obvious but frequently overlooked implications regarding the need for Church support of marriage and family life on the part of those concerned about the shortage of priests in the Church.[21]

The Latin American bishops wanted to discuss celibacy in the priesthood but Pope Paul vetoed the proposal. Earlier, a Brazilian bishop of Dutch descent got nowhere with his suggestion that the council discuss ordaining to the priesthood laymen who had been married at least five years for pastoral work in smaller congregations.

This final session also discussed and approved documents on Christian education and on the Church's attitudes toward non-Christian religions, which rejected anti-Semitism. The latter document said: "The Catholic Church rejects nothing that is true and holy in these religions."[22]

The council fathers finally approved the document on revelation, after some objections raised by a conservative appeal to the Council of Trent had been dealt with. They also approved progressive documents on the apostolate of the laity, on the life of priests, and, most significantly, the document on the Church in the modern world.

Both of the Vatican II constitutions on the Church (*Gaudium et Spes* and *Lumen Gentium*) discussed family life, and both gave the institutionalism of the Council of Trent a poke in the eye by recalling the ancient Church's conviction that the family is "the domestic church." As such, the family, not the parish, is the most basic unit of the Church. Yet it was not until the late 1970s that theologians began to understand the importance of this insight to the life of the Church as a whole. In recent years some local Church leaders have begun to realize that the health of the parish depends in great part on the health of the various kinds of families that constitute the parish, but many parishes still do not grasp its importance. Pastoral theologians have yet to begin a serious study of the implications of this strand of tradition for parishes and the Church as a whole.

The Second Vatican Council was a turning point in the history of the Catholic Church. It will be a long time, however, before anything resembling a final report card can be drawn up on Vatican II. "The impact of the Second Vatican Council," writes Hubert Jedin, "will. . . depend on whether the Church of the twentieth century renews itself in the spirit of Jesus Christ."[23]

The Current State of the Church

Any attempt to foretell the future of the Roman Catholic Church would be pure speculation. Faith can only trust in the promise Jesus makes to Peter in Matthew's Gospel: "And I tell you, you are Peter and on this rock I will build my church, and the gates of Hades will not prevail against it" (16:18).

In terms of specifics, we have the past to look at, which is what this book has been all about, and we can look around us at what is happening in the present. As it moves toward the dawn of the twenty-first century, the Catholic Church continues to flounder in the wake of the changes brought about in the mid-1960s by the Second Vatican Council. We may examine four aspects of the Church's life to see the current state of affairs, and from this one may attempt to extrapolate future directions if one chooses to do so. The four aspects of Church life are liturgy, leadership, spirituality, and ministry.

Liturgy

The Church's liturgy, the Eucharist, or Mass, is the heart of the Church's life. On the verge of the twenty-first century few observers would deny that liturgically the Church is on uncertain grounds. Most Catholics report satisfaction with the liturgical trends mapped out by Vatican II. They prefer the liturgy in their own language, for example.

At the same time there is widespread discontent with the quality of the liturgy in many parishes. Catholics frequently complain that the Eucharist is celebrated in a slapdash or pedestrian manner. It is not unusual for ordinary Catholics who grew up in the 1940s and 1950s to say that they miss the sense of mystery and transcendence that characterized the old Latin Mass. Still, most say that they would not want to return to the old Mass.

Among the parishes in a city of any size you will find progressive/liberal liturgies that go their own way with little concern for institutional directives, but you will also find more conservative/traditional parishes where the Eucharist is celebrated along more formal lines with strict attention paid to official Church liturgical directives. You will also find parishes at various points along the spectrum between the two extremes.

Liturgy has become a "do your own thing" project that each parish tries to deal with as best as it can. Sometimes it is well done, sometimes not. Liberal parishes allow liturgy committees more control than do conservative parishes.

To make things even more interesting, in the early 1990s, Pope John Paul II gave local bishops the authority to allow the celebration of the pre-Vatican II Latin Mass in parishes of their diocese. The result is that in dozens of parishes all over the United States, as well as in other countries, Catholics who wish to do so may attend an old-style Latin Mass. Parishes where Latin Masses are celebrated far outnumber those that celebrate the Mass only in English, and only according to the new rite. Still, it seems that any hope for liturgical unity, much less uniformity, in the Church is futile for the foreseeable future. Any Catholic living in a city of more than three or four parishes can find a liturgy with which he or she is comfortable, and the more parishes in a city the more options there are, from the old Latin Mass to a Mass designed to be "with it" in as many ways as possible.

Leadership

Catholic attitudes toward the Church's leadership, the pope, the bishops, and Vatican authorities also run the gamut from very conservative to very liberal. Sociological surveys indicate that since the 1968 publication of *Humanae Vitae*, the encyclical of Pope Paul VI best known for insisting that Catholic spouses may not use artificial contraceptives, the teaching authority of the papacy, particularly on issues related to human sexuality, has been seriously eroded. Conservative Catholics adhere to papal directives as if they came directly from God, while average to liberal Catholics don't pay much attention to statements from either the pope or other Vatican offices.

Yet the pope continues to hold a powerful place in the Catholic imagination, and papal visits to the United States are invariably major media events. The pope's appearances in huge sports stadiums are attended by many thousands of people.

There is much to be said for a papacy that serves as a focal point of unity and draws the attention of the whole world to significant issues. Even many non-Catholics appreciate it when a pope speaks out on important international issues. Only Catholicism has a figure like the pope who can capture the attention of so many people worldwide and address issues related to human and spiritual values. The idea of a papacy that can count on unquestioning obedience from most Catholics on every issue, however, does not seem to have much of a future.

Spirituality

Catholic spirituality, like every other dimension of Catholicism today, takes its understanding from the person's basic religious orientation, from liberal to conservative, from traditionalist to progressive. Progressives declare that spirituality is inseparable from the person's life as a whole. Conservatives prefer to speak of spirituality in explicitly formal religious terms. Progressives want to maintain connections between faith and everyday life, but they risk the loss of spirituality in the mundane. Conservatives want their faith to give them experiences of mystery and transcendence, but they risk compartmentalizing spirituality so it has little connection to everyday life.

Many, perhaps the majority, of Catholics don't give conscious attention to their spirituality most of the time. They think of it when they attend Mass on Sunday or Saturday evening. Perhaps they turn their attention to it now and

then in the course of an ordinary day. But for
the most part they pray when they attend Mass,
and that's about it. Like many people of other
faiths, Catholics are heavily influenced by a secular culture where spirituality has little if any
validity, and religion is supposed to be a personal matter on the same level as a hobby. One
is not supposed to bring one's religion into "the
real world," and if one does so it is considered in
bad taste.

Some Catholics, of course, do try to live
their faith as the foundation of their everyday
lives. They pray regularly, perhaps attend Mass
daily, and turn their attention often throughout
the day to the love of God present in the fabric
of their ordinary existence. Such an approach
to being Catholic is not easy, however, in a secular, pluralistic society.

Ministry

Probably the most significant ministry issue
Catholics face as they look ahead to the next
century is the steadily diminishing number of
priests available to serve parish communities.
More and more parishes find themselves shar-
ing a priest with other parishes or doing without a priest entirely, except for a visiting priest
who comes to celebrate the Eucharist, if they
are fortunate. Such parishes hire a lay person to

serve as "pastoral administrator" or some similar title. This leaves the parish without a priest to occupy the symbolic role of authority figure and liturgical leader.

Suggestions that married men and/or women be ordained to the priesthood are invariably rejected by the Vatican. This leads some to conclude that the Vatican places a higher value on male clerical celibacy than it does on making it possible for Catholic parishes to remain active eucharistic communities. As time goes by, it is possible that at least some Catholic parishes will lose touch with the Eucharist as the heart of Church life because they are unable to experience the Eucharist regularly.

At the same time, the growing scarcity of priests makes it necessary for laity to take responsibility for their parishes if they are to continue to function. In many parishes greater involvement on the part of lay men and women is a positive development that enables laity to "take ownership" of their parishes and shape them according to a faith for today and tomorrow.

* * *

The Catholic Church is in the midst of considerable turmoil and uncertainty as it prepares to move into a new century. It would, however, be a mistake to view turmoil and uncertainty as utterly negative characteristics of Church life. On the contrary, they are signs of life. If the

Church were dying it would look dead, but it does not. Turmoil and uncertainty are indications that countless people care about the Church and its future, they care enough about it to take positions, to argue, and to attend even poorly done liturgies and stick with their parishes.

Catholics love being Catholic, and they love their Church. Most wouldn't give up on being Catholic for anything. Therefore, the Catholic Church is alive and doing well. The future will bring what the future will bring, but for now the Church is thriving with never a dull moment.

Chapter 1. Jesus of Nazareth

1. Gerard Sloyan, *Jesus in Focus: A Life in Its Setting* (Mystic, Conn.: Twenty-Third Publications, 1983), 3.

2. Thomas Bokenkotter, *A Concise History of the Catholic Church* (New York: Doubleday & Co., 1977), 8.

3. See Raymond E. Brown, S.S., *The Churches the Apostles Left Behind* (Mahwah, N.J.: Paulist Press, 1984).

4. Xavier Léon-Dufour, S.J., *The Gospels and the Jesus of History* (New York: Doubleday Image Books, 1970), 28.

5. See especially Luke Timothy Johnson, *The Real Jesus: The Misguided Quest for the Historical Jesus and the Truth of the Traditional Gospels* (San Francisco: Harper San Francisco, 1996).

6. See Joseph A. Fitzmyer, S.J., *A Christological Catechism: New Testament Answers* (Mahwah, N.J.: Paulist Press, 1982), 16–17.

7. For information on the historical Jesus I rely on Fitzmyer, pp. 11–18, and Karl Baus, "From the Apostolic Community to Constantine," *History of the Church*, vol. 1, Hubert Jedin, ed. (New York: Crossroad Publishing, 1986).

8. Fitzmyer, 45.

9. Ibid., 46.

10. Baus, 72.

11. Jaroslav Pelikan, *Jesus Through the Centuries* (San Francisco: Harper & Row, 1987), 1.

CHAPTER 2. THE EARLY CHURCH

1. Pope John Paul II, *The Pope Speaks to the American Church* (San Francisco: Harper San Francisco, 1992), 223.

2. Thomas Bokenkotter, *A Concise History of the Catholic Church* (New York: Doubleday & Co., 1977), 26.

3. In her bestselling book, *Ten Stupid Things Women Do to Mess Up Their Lives* (New York: Villard Books, 1994), psychologist Dr. Laura Schlessinger calls cohabitation prior to marriage "the ultimate female self-delusion." See pp. 91–109. See also "Love and Marriage" in David G. Myers, *The Pursuit of Happiness* (New York: Avon Books, 1993), for statistics on the negative impact of cohabitation on subsequent marriages.

4. See John Evangelist Walsh, *The Bones of St. Peter: The First Full Account of the Search for the Apostle's Body* (New York: Doubleday & Co., 1982).

5. Quoted in Jean Comby, *How to Read Church History*, vol. 1, "From the Beginnings to the Fifteenth Century" (New York: Crossroad Publishing, 1985), 40.

CHAPTER 3. THE CHURCH GIVES BIRTH TO THE NEW TESTAMENT

1. James L. Megivern, *Official Catholic Teachings: Bible Interpretation* (Wilmington, N.C.: McGrath Publishing Co., 1978), 393.

2. See Luke Timothy Johnson, *The Real Jesus: The Misguided Quest for the Historical Jesus and the Truth of the Traditional Gospels* (San Francisco: Harper San Francisco, 1996), 81–104.

3. John H. Hayes and Carl R. Holladay, *Biblical Exegesis: A Beginner's Handbook* (Atlanta, Ga.: John Knox Press, 1982), 95.

4. Raymond E. Brown, S. S., *The Churches the Apostles Left Behind* (Mahwah, N.J.: Paulist Press, 1984), 128.

5. For the remainder of this chapter I rely on: James C. Turro and Raymond E. Brown, S.S., "Canonicity," in *The Jerome Biblical Commentary* (Eastwood Cliffs, N.J.: Prentice-Hall, 1968); "Canonization," in *Introduction to the New Testament*, by Raymond F. Collins (New York: Doubleday & Co., 1983); and "The Formation of the Canon of the New Testament," in Werner Georg Kümmel, *Introduction to the New Testament* (Nashville, Tenn.: Abingdon Press, 1981).

6. The words in quotation marks are those of the Council of Trent, quoted in Megivern, 179.

7. Turro and Brown, 534.

Chapter 4. The Constantinian Era

1. Eusebius, *The Ecclesiastical History*, ed. and trans. K. Lake and J.E.L. Oulton, vol. 2 (London: Loeb Classical Library, 1932), 359–65.

2. Ibid., 360.

3. Lactantius, *On the Deaths of the Persecutors*, ed. Jacques Moreau (Paris, 1954), 126–28. Translated by John W. Eadie, in *The Conversion of Constantine*, ed. by John W. Eadie (New York: Robert E. Krieger, 1977), 11–12.

4. Ibid., 11.

5. Ibid., 12.

6. Eusebius, *Life of Constantine,* trans. E.C. Richardson, in *A Select Library of Nicene and Post-Nicene Fathers of the Christian Church,* 2nd ser., vol. 1 (New York, 1890), 489–93.

7. Ibid., 490.

8. Leo Donald Davis, S.J., *The First Seven Ecumenical Councils (325–787): Their History and Theology* (Wilmington, Del.: Michael Glazier, 1987), 29.

9. Thomas Bokenkotter, *A Concise History of the Catholic Church,* rev. and exp. ed. (New York: Doubleday Image Books, 1990), 39.

10. Davis, 58.

11. Ibid., 51.

12. Ibid., 60.

CHAPTER 5. THE COUNCIL OF CHALCEDON

1. Jean Comby, *How to Read Church History,* vol. 1, "From the Beginnings to the Fifteenth Century" (New York: Crossroad Publishing, 1985), 96–97.

2. Socrates, *Church History,* VII, 34, quoted in Comby, 96.

3. Ibid.

4. Comby, 97.

5. Socrates, quoted in Comby, 96.

6. Ibid.

7. Ibid.

8. Ibid.

9. Ibid., 97.

10. Leo Donald Davis, S.J., *The First Seven Ecumenical Councils (325–787): Their History and Theology* (Wilmington, Del.: Michael Glazier, 1987), 178.

11. Thomas Bokenkotter, *A Concise History of the Catholic Church*, rev. and exp. ed. (New York: Doubleday Image Books, 1990), 83.
12. Davis, 175.
13. Comby, 99.
14. Quoted in Comby, 98.
15. Frederick J. Cwiekowski, *The Beginnings of the Church* (Mahwah, N.J.: Paulist Press, 1988), 62–63.
16. John C. Dwyer, *Church History*, vol. 5 (New York: Crossroad Publishing, 1985), 5.
17. Ibid., 106.
18. Davis, 194.

CHAPTER 6. THE CRUSADES, THE INQUISITION, SAINT DOMINIC, AND SAINT FRANCIS OF ASSISI

1. Anthony E. Gilles, *The People of the Faith* (Cincinnati, Ohio: St. Anthony Messenger, 1982), 91.
2. Ibid., 97.
3. Carl Koch, *A Popular History of the Catholic Church* (Winona, Minn.: St. Mary's Press, 1997), 151.
4. John Jay Hughes, *Pontiffs: Popes Who Shaped History* (Huntington, Ind.: Our Sunday Visitor, 1994), 102.
5. Koch, 149.
6. Hubert Jedin, ed., *History of the Church*, vol. 4 (New York: Crossroad Publishing, 1982), 212.

CHAPTER 7. THE PROTESTANT REFORMATION

1. Hubert Jedin, ed., *History of the Church*, vol. 5 (New York: Crossroad Publishing, 1986), 5.
2. Ibid., 6.

3. Anthony E. Gilles, *The People of Anguish: The Story Behind the Reformation* (Cincinnati, Ohio: St. Anthony Messenger, 1987), 33.

4. Jedin, 7.

5. Thomas Bokenkotter, *A Concise History of the Catholic Church,* rev. and exp. ed. (New York: Doubleday Image Books, 1990), 180.

6. Ibid.

7. John M. Todd, *Luther: A Life* (New York: Crossroad Publishing, 1983), 1.

8. See Roland H. Bainton, *Erasmus of Christendom* (New York: Crossroad Publishing, 1982).

9. Jedin, 13.

10. This translation is from the *New American Bible,* Revised Edition.

11. John C. Dwyer, *Church History: Twenty Centuries of Catholic Christianity* (Mahwah, N.J.: Paulist Press, 1985), 229.

12. Ibid., 233.

CHAPTER 8. THE COUNCIL OF TRENT

1. John C. Dwyer, *Church History: Twenty Centuries of Catholic Christianity* (Mahwah, N.J.: Paulist Press, 1985), 276.

2. Anthony E. Gilles, *The People of Anguish: The Story Behind the Reformation* (Cincinnati, Ohio: St. Anthony Messenger, 1987), 114.

3. Hubert Jedin, "Council of Trent," in *The New Catholic Encyclopedia,* vol. 14 (New York: McGraw-Hill, 1967), 272.

4. Richard P. McBrien, *Catholicism* (San Francisco: Harper San Francisco, 1994), 14.

5. Jedin, 273.

6. Thomas Bokenkotter, *A Concise History of the Catholic Church*, rev. and exp. ed. (New York: Doubleday Image Books, 1990), 218.

7. *American Catholic Family*, vol. 1, no. 2, p. 1. The information on the implicit antifamily drift of the Counter-Reformation in the following paragraphs is based on material in this issue. See also Mitch and Kathy Finley, *Building Christian Families* (Allen, Tex.: Thomas More Publications, 1996), and Mitch Finley, *Your Family in Focus: Appreciating What You Have, Making It Even Better* (Notre Dame, Ind.: Ave Maria Press, 1994).

8. John Paul II, *Familiaris Consortio*, no. 70. See also *The Pope Speaks to the American Church* (San Francisco: Harper San Francisco, 1992), where John Paul II says: "The priests and their collaborators in a parish must try to be very close to all families in their need for pastoral care, and to provide the support and nourishment they require," 223.

9. See Ad Hoc Commission on Marriage and Family Life, National Conference of Catholic Bishops, *A Family Perspective in Church and Society* (Washington, D.C.: Office of Publishing and Promotion Services, United States Catholic Conference, 1988). See also *Follow the Way of Love: A Pastoral Message of the U.S. Catholic Bishops to Families* (Washington, D.C.: Office for Publishing and Promotion Services, United States Catholic Conference, 1994).

Chapter 9. Ultramontanism and the First Vatican Council

1. Roger Aubert et al., "The Church in the Age of Liberalism," in Hubert Jedin, ed., *History of the Church*, vol. 8 (New York: Crossroad Publishing, 1981), 83.

2. Ibid., 84.

3. Thomas Bokenkotter, *A Concise History of the Catholic Church*, rev. and exp. ed. (New York: Doubleday Image Books, 1990), 268.

4. The term *ultramontanism* means "of or pertaining to territory beyond the mountains, especially the Alps." In effect, the term seems to refer to the fact that ultramontanism originated in locations distant from Rome.

5. Aubert et al., 304.

6. John C. Dwyer, *Church History: Twenty Centuries of Catholic Christianity* (Mahwah, N.J.: Paulist Press, 1985), 334.

7. Ibid., 362.

8. Ibid., 340.

9. Peter Hebblethwaite, *Pope John XXIII: Shepherd of the Modern World* (New York: Doubleday & Co., 1985), 465.

10. Aubert et al., 318.

11. Bokenkotter, 280.

12. Dwyer, 345.

13. Bokenkotter, 305.

14. J. Derek Holmes and Bernard W. Bickers, *A Short History of the Catholic Church* (Mahwah, N.J.: Paulist Press, 1984), 243.

Chapter 10. Pius X and the Modernist Crisis

1. Roger Aubert et al., "The Church in the Industrial Age," in Hubert Jedin, ed., *History of the Church,* vol. 9 (New York: Crossroad Publishing, 1981), 420.

2. J. Derek Holmes and Bernard W. Bickers, *A Short History of the Catholic Church* (Mahwah, N.J.: Paulist Press, 1984), 254.

3. Thomas Bokenkotter, *A Concise History of the Catholic Church,* rev. and exp. ed. (New York: Doubleday Image Books, 1990), 319.

4. Note that in 1996 Pope John Paul II formally announced that the Catholic Church sees no necessary conflict between Darwin's theory of evolution and the belief that God created human beings.

5. Aubert et al., 421.

6. John C. Dwyer, *Church History: Twenty Centuries of Catholic Christianity* (Mahwah, N.J.: Paulist Press, 1985), 362.

7. Ibid.

8. Ibid.

9. Quoted in Aubert et al., 434.

10. See "Instruction of Pontifical Biblical Commission Concerning the Historical Truth of the Gospels," in James L. Megivern, ed., *Official Catholic Teachings: Bible Interpretation* (Wilmington, N.C.: McGrath Publishing Co., 1978), 391–98.

11. Anthony E. Gilles, *The People of Hope: The Story Behind the Modern Church* (Cincinnati, Ohio.: St. Anthony Messenger, 1988), 70.

12. Ibid.

13. Aubert et al., 442.

14. Gilles, 70.

15. Bokenkotter, 319.

16. Aubert et al., 467.

17. Ibid.

18. Ibid.

19. The consensus among both Catholic and mainline Protestant Scripture scholars today is that Moses did not write the Pentateuch—the first five books of the Old Testament—that Isaiah was written by two or three authors, that Mark was the first Gospel to be written, and that Saint Paul did not write the Letter to the Hebrews.

20. Aubert et al., 468.

21. Ibid., 471.

22. For the information in this section on John XXIII, I gratefully acknowledge my dependence on Chapter 4 of the outstanding biography by Peter Hebblethwaite, *Pope John XXIII: Shepherd of the Modern World* (New York: Doubleday & Co., 1985).

23. Ibid., 74.

24. Ibid., 75.

25. John Henry Cardinal Newman, *An Essay on the Development of Christian Doctrine* (Westminster, Md.: Christian Classics, 1968 [original edition, 1845]), 177.

CHAPTER 11. JOHN XXIII AND THE SECOND VATICAN COUNCIL

1. Gabriel Adrianyi et al., *History of the Church*, vol. 10, "The Church in the Modern Age," Hubert Jedin, ed.

and author of section quoted in this chapter (New York: Crossroad Publishing, 1981), 98.

2. Adrianyi et al., 99.

3. John Jay Hughes, "The Council and the Synod: A Tale of Two Popes," *St. Anthony Messenger* (October 1985), 16; quoted in Anthony E. Gilles, *The People of Hope: The Story Behind the Modern Church* (Cincinnati, Ohio: St. Anthony Messenger, 1988), 324.

4. Quoted in Peter Hebblethwaite, *Pope John XXIII: Shepherd of the Modern World* (New York: Doubleday & Co., 1985), 324.

5. Ibid., 431.

6. Ibid., 435.

7. John C. Dwyer, *Church History: Twenty Centuries of Catholic Christianity* (Mahwah, N.J.: Paulist Press, 1985), 387.

8. Quoted in Hebblethwaite, 432.

9. Ibid.

10. Adrianyi et al., 107.

11. Ibid., 108.

12. Thomas Bokenkotter, *A Concise History of the Catholic Church*, rev. and exp. ed. (New York: Doubleday Image Books, 1990), 359.

13. Quoted in Hebblethwaite, 411.

14. Ibid., 504.

15. Adrianyi et al., 114.

16. Ibid., 116.

17. Ibid., 117.

18. Quoted in Hebblethwaite, 344.

19. See Robert Blair Kaiser, *The Politics of Sex and Religion* (Kansas City, Mo.: Sheed & Ward, 1985), and Robert

McClory, *Turning Point: The Inside Story of the Papal Birth Control Commission and How Humanae Vitae Changed the Life of Patty Crowley and the Future of the Church* (New York: Crossroad Publishing, 1995).

20. Bokenkotter, 385.
21. Adrianyi et al., 138.
22. Ibid.
23. Ibid., 151.

INDEX

Acton, as uniting opponents of ultramontanism, 181

Acts of the Apostles
  acceptance as Scripture of, 55
  community of the disciples and idealized early Church in, 20
  daily gathering of disciples in Temple described in, 24
  history of Pentecost in, 20–21
  Peter as leader of Jerusalem community in, 23

Adrian VI, sin of Church hierarchy noted by, 124

Albert of Magdeburg, punishment for heretics decreed by, 113

Albigensians, 108–10

Albrecht of Brandenburg, fees for archbishop position of, 131–33

Antioch
  Jesus' humanity stressed by theologians in, 82
  spread of Christianity among non-Jewish people in, 25–26

Apologists, 31

Arianism, as debated at First Council of Nicaea, 72–77

Arius, heresy of, 74, 76

Aubert, Roger
  secret antimodernist integralist organization described by, 207
  ultramontane movement described by, 170
  view of Pius IX of, 168

Augustine of Hippo, Luther's interpretation of, 151
Aurelius, Marcus, 32

Baptism
   apologists' description of, 31
   catechumenate as preparation for, 36
   decision at Council of Jerusalem about prerequisites
      for, 26–27
   effects on family life of Church legislation on, 157
   as one of two sacraments for Martin Luther, 151
Baronius, Cesare, 208
Baus, Karl
   description of Jesus by, 8
   theme of Jesus' teaching described by, 11
Beatitudes, 48
Benedict XV, denunciation as modernist of, 210
Benedictine communities, corruption at time of Protestant
      Reformation, 125–26
Bernard of Clairvaux, crusade called by, 103–4
Bishop of Rome
   empowerment by mid-fifth century of, 92
   as presiding over Church councils, 83, 89–90
Bishops
   absenteeism of, 147
   appointment of, 77, 172–73
   arrest and execution by Licinius of, 64
   condescension prior to Protestant Reformation of, 123
   control over dioceses granted to, 160
   divine origins of office of, 178

guidance as authorities in early Church by, 34

Inquisitions organized by local, 113–14

Nestorius condemned as heretic by, 84–85

opposition to papal infallibility of, 180–81

origins in early Church of, 30, 37

participation in First Council of Nicaea of, 73, 76, 77

at Second Vatican Council, 224

Bokenkotter, Thomas

alliance of Church with state in Roman Empire analyzed by, 71

antimodernist encyclical described by, 202–3

Catholic scholarship as suppressed by antimodernism according to, 204

corruption during Protestant Reformation noted by, 126–27

early Church as remaining Jewish according to, 23

implications of Tridentine Mass described by, 154–55

purpose of Gospels for, 2–3

Second Vatican Council described by, 226, 234

ultramontanes at First Vatican Council described by, 180

Book of Revelation

as debated for inclusion in New Testament, 52–55

relative importance of, 56

Borromeo, Charles, 157

Bossy, John, 156–57

Brown, Raymond

conflicts in New Testament text analyzed by, 51

disagreements of Bible with modern times analyzed by, 57

Calvin, John, 147

Cardinals

appointed to carry out Council of Trent's decrees, 166

Carollanti, A., antimodernist writings of, 205–6

Catholic Church

Bible deemphasized by, 151

change in, *xvii*

current state of, 239–46

development of caste system in, 71–72

divorce rate, 27

early, 19–38

foundational events of, 19–20, 42–43, 56

history of, understanding, *xiv–xix*

institutional developments of, 37–38

liturgy of, 240–41

outdated claims during Protestant Reformation of, 123

parish as center of Catholic religious life, 156

reform efforts within, 140

spirituality of today, 243–44

split between Rome (Roman Catholic) and Constantinople (Orthodox) of, 65, 82, 96–97, 119

turmoil in today's, 245–46

Celestine, condemnation of Nestorius by, 83

Celibacy, 245

vetoed from discussion at Second Vatican Council, 235–36

Celsus, *True Discourse* written by, 31

Central America, persecution of Christians in, 35–36

Chalcedonian doctrine, 92–94, 96

Charles V

protest at moving council by, 145–46

reconciliation of Catholic and Protestant churches attempted by, 144–45

Trent suggested as locale of council by, 144

Christian communities, early

background of converts in, 25–28

as existing before Christian sacred writings were compiled, 41

persecution of Christians by Rome, 28, 31–32, 34–36, 38

preservation of documents for New Testament by, 52–53

Christianity

acceptance as official religion of Roman Empire of, 71

beginning of, 19

legalization of, 61

as questioned following Second Crusade, 104

Christians

assemblies of early, 43

edict of toleration by Gallerius for, 38

penance and reconciliation for returning, 37

persecution of early, 31–36, 38, 48, 64

prayers developed by early, 29–30

values and attitudes of others for, 13

Cicero, Marcus Tullius, *xiv*

Comby, Jean, Cyril of Alexandria's doctrine described by, 83

Concerning the Historical Truth of the Gospels (Pontifical Biblical Commission), 43–44

Confessional box, introduction of, 157

Conrad III, crusade led by, 104

Constantine (Flavius Valerius Aurelius Constantinus)

  accounts of conversion of, 65–67

  baptism on deathbed of, 70–71

  birth and family background of, 61–62

  conversion to Christianity of, 65–70

  declaration as emperor of, 62

  decrees of First Council of Nicaea confirmed by, 77

  First Council of Nicaea called by, 72

  freedom for Christians aided by laws of, 62–63, 65

  legalization of Christianity by, 61

  pagan worship abolished by, 63

  sainthood in Eastern Orthodox Church of, 71

  significance of, 72

  victory over Licinius of, 64

  victory over Maxentius at Milvian Bridge of, 62, 65–69

Constantinople

  attack during Crusades of, 102, 106–7

  as new center of Roman empire, 65

"Constitution on the Infallible Teaching Authority of the Roman Pontiff," 183–84

Constitution on the Sacred Liturgy, approval of, 232

Constitutions on the Church of Second Vatican Council (*Gaudium et Spes* and *Lumen Gentium*), 236

Converts, gentile

  doctrinal controversy about, 25–26

  problems in understanding Jewish religion and culture of, 44–45

Converts, Jewish, explanations of Jesus as fulfilling Jewish traditions for, 45

Corruption
    in Church of prior to Protestant Reformation, 120, 123
    condemnation by Martin Luther of, 131
    among clergy and in monasteries during minor crusades, 108

Council of Basel (1431), power and money surrendered by Martin V for, 122

Council of Chalcedon (451), 81–97
    as called by Marcion, 89–90
    Chalcedonian doctrine developed at, 92–94
    opening of, 90

Council of Constantinople (381), 91

Council of Ephesus (430), 83–86

Council of Ephesus, second (449), 87–89

Council of Jerusalem (49), 26–27

Council of Trent (1545–63), 139–61
    answers to Martin Luther's criticisms by, 149
    antifamily bias after, 157–58, 160
    Catholic Church's version of Scriptures decided by, 150
    closing of, 155
    finality of split of Luther and Church caused by, 139–40
    hierarchical nature of Church reaffirmed by, 151–52
    marriage decrees of, 148
    New Testament contents approved at, 56
    obstacles to, 141, 142
    outcomes of, 156–57, 160

papacy as reformed by, 127

Protestant Reformation as causing call to, 136, 156

reaffirmation of seven sacraments by, 151

reform of Mass by, 152–53

Second Vatican Council's break with, 227, 236

seminary training for priests required by, 159

sessions of, 144–45

Counter-Reformation, parish as core of Catholic faith life during, 158

Crusades, 102–8

advances in knowledge and trade during, 108

Children's Crusade during, 107

First of major, 102–3

Fourth of major, 105–7

Muslim casualties during, 102–3, 105

Muslim control of Holy Land, 107

people's perceptions of Christianity changed by, 101–2

and Richard the Lionhearted during Third Crusade, 104–5

Saladin, English prisoners killed by, 105

Second of major, 103–4

Third of major, 104–5

Curia, Vatican

as attempting to control Second Vatican Council, 225–26, 229

John XXIII at, 218

simony by, 121

Cyril of Alexandria

Council of Ephesus opened by, 83

unity of Christ defended by, 82–83, 91

Darwin, Charles, 192

Davis, Leo Donald
  Arius described by, 74
  Constantine's conversion analyzed by, 70
  effect of Chalcedonian doctrine described by, 96
  second Council of Ephesus described by, 88–89

Deacons
  appointment of early, 30
  relation to bishops of early, 37

Decius, persecution of Christians by, 35

Diocletian
  persecution of Christians by, 38
  Tetrarchy begun by, 62

Dioscoros of Alexandria, 87–88, 90–91

Disciples of Jesus
  experience of risen Christ by, 20
  history of, 9–10
  as leaders selected by Jesus, 22
  persecution of, 24

Divino Afflante Spiritu, 233

Dominicans (Order of Preachers)
  approved by Innocent III, 111–12
  corruption during Protestant Reformation of, 126
  evolution into scholars of, 112
  mendicant lifestyle of, 110
  primary purpose of preaching for, 110–11

Dupanloup, Félix, interpretation of Pius IX's *Syllabus*
    by, 176

Dwyer, John C.
  Chalcedonian doctrine described by, 94–95

development of doctrine recounted by, 196–97

Martin Luther's insight noted by, 130

papal infallibility beliefs described by, 178, 182

response to reforms proposed at Council of Trent noted by, 140

unification of seminary instruction described by, 173

Early Church, 19–38

  bishops in, 34

  Christian faith distinguished from Mosaic Law in, 25–27

  Eucharist in, 21

  oral tradition about Jesus in, 44–45

  presbyters in, 30, 37–38

  rejection of extremes by, 34

Easter, establishment of observance for, 76

Eastern Orthodox Church

  destruction of possibility for reconciliation between Roman Catholics and, 102, 106–7

  split between Roman Catholic Church and, 65, 82, 96–97, 119

Eastern Rite Churches, 179

Eck, Johannes, 134

Enlightenment, 189–90

Erasmus of Rotterdam

  corruption in Church reported by, 126

  need for reform in Church described by, 127

Erbach, Dietrich von, 125

Eucharist

   for early Church members, 21

   evolution of, 37

   First Council of Nicaea as setting rule of standing
     for, 77

   formality of, 241

   as one of two sacraments for Martin Luther, 151

Eusebius, 66–68

Eutyches, 87, 88

Fabian, execution of, 35

Faith

   presentation and substance separated by John
     XXIII for, 222

   scientific methods as not needed to justify, 199

Family

   bias after Council of Trent against, 157–58, 160

   new Catholic turn to, 160–61, 237

   support of Second Vatican Council for, 235–36

Ferrari, Andrea, 206

First Council of Nicaea (324–325), 72–77, 86

   appointment of bishops established at, 77

   Arianism debated at, 72–73

   closing of, 77

   Nicene Creed developed at, 74–76

   observance of Easter established at, 76

   rules of living for clerics set at, 77

   standing during Eucharist established at, 77

First Vatican Council, 165–85
  closing of, 184
  opening of, 179
  outcomes of, 183–84
  papal infallibility as main subject at, 180–85
  and Pius IX, 172–73, 178
  representation at, 179
  Roman Catholic Church shaped by, 165
  state of Pius IX at, 179
Fitzmyer, Joseph, description of Jesus by, 8–11
Francis Bernadone (Francis of Assisi)
  friars as followers of, 110
  impoverished lifestyle of, 111
  new approach of, 102
Franciscans
  approved by Innocent III, 111–12
  corruption during Protestant Reformation of, 126
  evolution into scholars of, 112
  as inspired by Francis of Assisi, 111
  mendicant lifestyle of, 110
Frederick I of Germany during Third Crusade, 104–5
Freud, Sigmund, 192

Gallerius, edict of toleration for Christians in 311 by, 38
  persecutions of Christians in third century by, 35
Gilles, Anthony E.
  central ideas of modernism described by, 200–1
  Dominicans and Franciscans described by, 110
  revival by Paul IV of Inquisition described by, 146–47

Second Crusade described by, 105

view of Leo X of, 124

Gnosticism

and *Demiurge* deity, 32

as heresy within Church, 32

revival of version of, 108–9

Gospel of John

acceptance as Scripture of, 55

Jesus' historical presence and human nature in, 7

representation of resurrection in, 14

writing of, 44, 46–48, 49

Gospel of Luke

acceptance as Scripture of, 55

portrayal of Jesus in, 3–4

representation of resurrection in, 14

writing of, 44, 46–49

Gospel of Mark

acceptance as Scripture of, 55

representation of resurrection in, 14

writing of, 44, 46–48

Gospel of Matthew

acceptance as Scripture of, 55

law on earth described in, 51

portrayal of Jesus in, 3–4

representation of resurrection in, 14

writing of, 44, 46–48

Gospel of Peter

acceptance as Scripture of, 55

as rejected for New Testament, 53

Gregory VII, papal infallibility decreed by, 171, 180

Gregory IX, Inquisition ordered by, 109, 114–15
Gregory XVI, stubbornness against change of, 170
Guzman, Dominic (Saint Dominic)
   Dominicans founded by, 110–11
   friars as followers of, 110

Hayes, John H., 47
Hebrew Scriptures. *See* Old Testament
Heresy
   of Alfred Loisy, 198
   of Arius, 74, 76
   Gnosticism as, 32
   Inquisition as concerned with eliminating, 112–16
   in Middle Ages, 113
   punishments for, 115
Holladay, Carl R., 47
Holy Office, criticism of approach of, 232
Holy Spirit
   as at work during Second Vatican Council, 224, 231
   working of, *xviii*
Hughes, John Jay, 111
Humanae Vitae, 242

Ignatius of Antioch, 30
Immaculate Conception of Mary, 173–74, 177
Indulgences
   of Albrecht of Brandenburg, 131–33
   confirmation of Council of Trent for, 148–49

Infancy Gospel of Thomas, 53–54

Innocent III

    approval of Franciscan and Dominican orders by, 111

    military campaign against Albigensians by, 109–10

    plan for Christendom including Holy Land by, 105–6

Inquisition, 112–16

    bishops as organizing, 113–14

    friars used as instruments of, 112

    as ordered by Gregory IX, 109

    revived by Paul IV, 146–47

Islam, strengthening of hold on the East during Crusades

    of, 107

Jedin, Hubert, *xiv, xvii–xvix*

    anecdotes of John XXIII noted by, 218

    mourning of John XXIII described by, 228

    Second Vatican Council summarized by, 237

Jerusalem

    early Church of, 23

    German emperor's control of, 107

    Muslim control of, as cause of Crusades, 103–6

Jesus of Nazareth, 1–15

    adapting stories about, 6–7

    awareness of himself of, 7

    beginning of teaching and preaching by, 9

    historical, 6, 8, 44

    oral tradition in early Church about life and teachings

        of, 44–45

    physical appearance of, 7–8

representation in Gospels of, 3–4, 48–49

teaching of, 10–13

union of divinity and humanity in, 82–87, 91–95

Word of God as human being in, *xv*, 49

Jews

as first to receive message of Gospel, 24

murdered during Crusades, 102, 103

John of Antioch, Cyril of Alexandria condemned by,
85, 86

John the Baptist, 9

John Paul II

family as basic unit of the Church for, 22

Tridentine Mass allowed by, 154, 241

John XXIII, *xv*, 215–37

Biblical Commission chastised by, 227

biographical background of, 216

as bishop, 217

as cardinal, 217, 218

conservative decisions by, 223

death during Second Vatican Council of, 228

deathblow to antimodernism by, 221

as denounced by integralists, 208–9

election as pope of, 218–19

as military chaplain, 216–17

piety of, 217–18

pontificate of, 215

at Roman Curia, 218

Second Vatican Council called by, 219–20

teaching work of, 216

Johnson, Luke Timothy, description of Jesus by, 8

Johnson, Samuel, *xiii*

Julius III, efforts at church reform by, 146

Judas Iscariot, 10, 30

Justin Martyr

as early apologist, 31

execution of, 32

Kempis, Thomas à, reform attempts by, 127

Kierkegaard, Søren, 193

Koch, Carl, fear of heresy in Middle Ages described by, 112–13

Lactantius, account of Constantine's conversion by, 67–68

Laity, maturation during Protestant Reformation of, 123

Latin Catholicism, customs and devotions of, 140

Leo (bishop of Rome)

condemnation of second Council of Ephesus by, 89

representatives sent to Council of Chalcedon by, 90

union of divine and human natures of Christ expressed in *Tome* by, 87, 91–92

Leo X

corruption and neglect of, 124, 131–32

as savior of Reformation, 122

Leo XII, endorsement of Thomas Aquinas' philosophy by, 193–94

Leo XIII
  antimodernism of, 192–94
  condemnation of Alfred Loisy by, 198
  errors or contradictions in Bible explained by, 194
Léon-Dufour, Xavier, 6
Letter of Jude, 54
Letter to Philemon, 54
Letter to the Hebrews
  authorship of, 50
  as debated for inclusion in New Testament, 52
Letter to the Romans
  Martin Luther's reaction to, 130
  relative importance of, 56
Letters of Obscure Men, The, 126
Licinius
  execution of, 65
  harassment of Christians by, 64
  leadership of eastern provinces of Roman empire by, 62
  victory of Constantine over, 64
Life of Constantine, 68–70
Loisy, Alfred
  historical methods of theological study used by, 197–99
  popes' condemnation of, 198, 199
Longfellow, Henry Wadsworth, *xiii*
Lord's Supper, Jesus' instructions about continuing, 14
Louis VII, call for crusade by, 104
Luther, Martin, 120
  Council of Trent as answering criticisms by, 149, 156
  debate of ideas of, 134
  education of, 128, 130

excommunication document for, 135
family background of, 128
fear of God of, 130–31
Luder, Hans (father of Martin Luther), 128
Ninety-five Theses of, 132–33
personal encounter with God of, 131
pope as ignoring calls for reform by, 122
popular response to, 123, 127–28
religious vows as monk of, 129
salvation for, roots of, 151
theological ideas of, 135, 151

McBrien, Richard, 150
Marcion (c. 110–60), as early heretic, 33
Marriage, roots of legalistic view of, 148
Martin V, payment for Council of Basel by, 122
Mary, mother of Jesus
    debate at Church council about term *Theotokos* for,
        82, 85, 86
    history of, 9
Mass
    medieval, 153
    payments for, 125
    reformed by Council of Trent, 152–53
    sacrificial character of, 152
    sale of, 153
    transubstantiation during, 152
    Tridentine, 154–55
    use of Latin, 154

Matthias, 30

Merton, Thomas, *xv*

Middle Ages

Church during, 101–16

clerical monopoly over schools during, 122–23

Modernist crisis, 189–211

central ideas causing, 200–201

defined, 190–91

rejection of obedience of Roman authorities during, 191

Monks and monasticism

Cistercian monasteries, virtue and integrity of, 125

corruption during minor crusades among, 108

corruption during Protestant Reformation of, 126

mendicant, 110–12

Monophysitism, 95–96

Montalembert, liberal Catholicism defended by, 174–75

Montanus, Jesus' return announced by, 33, 34

Mosaic Law

Christian faith distinguished in early Church from, 25–27

First Council of Nicaea, 76–77

Muratorian Fragment, 54

Nazis, persecutions of Christians by, 35–36

Neo-ultramontanism, 177

Nestorianism, 95–96

Nestorius of Constantinople, debate about Mary of, 82–86

"New Syllabus of Errors" of Holy Office, 201–2

New Testament, 41–57

  acceptance and rejection of documents for, 52–56

  historical character of, 42

  history of Jesus in, 1–3

  nonhistorical material in, 4–5

  shaping of, 43, 51–52

  writers of, 2–3, 50–52

Newman, John Henry, denunciation of antimodernist thought by, 210–11

Nicene Creed

  adoption by Monophysites of, 96

  development at First Council of Nicaea of, 74–76

  phrases added at Council of Constantinople to, 91

Nicholas of Myra, origins of Santa Claus in, 73

Ninety-five Theses, 132–33

Old Testament

  compilation and approval of, 41

  references of early Christians to, 41–42

Order of Preachers. *See* Dominicans

Ottaviani, document on the Church at Second Vatican Council headed by, 231–32

Papal infallibility, 171–73, 177

  basis for, 179

  discussion at First Vatican Council of, 181–82

Guidi as making compromise regarding, 182

as main subject at First Vatican Council, 180–85

problems caused by doctrine of, 185

Papal Inquisition, 109, 114–15

Paul

Christ as end of Law for, 51

distinction between Christian faith and Mosaic Law
by, 25–27

execution of, 28

imprisonment of, 28

letters of and to, 50, 55

missionary journeys of, 27–28

Paul III, reform of Church started by, 141–44

Paul IV

approach to Protestant-Catholic split of, 145, 146

Inquisition revived by, 146–47

Paul VI

encyclical against artificial contraceptive use of, 242

interventions to pacify conservatives by, 233–34

Second Vatican Council continued by, 229

Pelikan, Jaroslav, 15

Pentecost

accounts in Acts of, 20–21

as birth of Church, 43

Peter

burial place of, 28–29

chastisement by Paul about gentile Christians of, 26

at Council of Jerusalem, 26–27

execution of, 28

as leader described in Paul's letters and in Acts, 23
   letters to, 50
Philip the Arab, 35
Phillip II of France during Second Crusade, 104–5
Pilate, Pontius, 10
Pius IV
   conciliar approach to Catholic-Protestant split of, 145
   and Council of Trent, 147
Pius IX *(Pio Nono)*
   accomplishments of, 184
   condemnation of liberalism by, 174
   at First Vatican Council, 179
   as supporter of ultramontanism, 170–73, 182, 184
   Syllabus of Errors encyclical on "errors" of the day by,
      175–76, 178
Pius X
   achievements of, 195
   antimodernist oath required for educators by, 204
   campaign against modernism of, 196, 199–205
   canonization of, 195–96
   condemnation of Alfred Loisy by, 199
   death of, 209
   encyclical structuring modernism issued by, 202–3
   support of integralists by, 206–7
   ultramontane battle taken up by, 194–95
Pius XII
   and antimodernism, 195
   encyclical accepting modern historical methods of, 233
   John XXIII appointed cardinal by, 217

Pliny the Younger, 29

Popes

antimodernism of, 190–92, 195–96, 203–6, 221

as autocrats following Council of Trent, 166

as bishops of Rome, 30

as cause of Protestant Reformation, 120, 126–27

defense of papal states as primary interest of, 167

doctrinal decisions of, 183

infallibility of, 171–73, 177, 179–85

place in Catholic imagination today of, 242–43

power granted by Council of Trent to, 159

reform required after Protestant Reformation from, 141

social upheavals ignored by, 167

Priests

cohabitation of, 123

condescension prior to Protestant Reformation of, 123

corruption during minor crusades of, 108

decline in number of, 244–45

liturgical eccentricities of, 153

origins as presbyters in early Church of, 30, 37–38

as responsible for catechetical formation of children, 156

seminary training required after Council of Trent for, 159

Protestant Reformation. *See* Reformation, Protestant

Q document, as source for Gospels, 47

Qoheleth, *xiv*

Rahner, Karl, revolutionary phases in Church described
    by, *xvi*
Redaction of Gospels, 46–49
Reformation, Protestant, 119–36. *See also* Luther, Martin
    causes of, 120
    corruption in Church at time of, 120, 123, 125–27
    Council of Trent as response to, 136, 156
    maturation of laity during, 123
Reign of Terror, 167
Resurrection, treatment in Gospels of, 14–15, 42–43, 49
Revised Roman Missal, rubrics of, 153
Roncalli, Angelo Giuseppe. *See* John XXIII

Sacraments, *xviii*, 151
Saint Peter's Basilica in Rome
    completion of, 132
    John XXIII's arrival to Second Vatican Council at,
        220–21
    Second Vatican Council as gathered in nave of, 224
Saladin, 105
Salvation
    effects of Church legislation on baptism, 157
    Jesus' teachings about, 11
    meaning of, 43
Scientific and historical methods
    applied to traditional faith by modernists, 190–98
    Catholic academic circles as open to, 193
    denounced by popes, 198, 199–200

Second Vatican Council (1962–65), 215–37
  bishops attending, 224
  curia as attempting to control, 225–26, 229
  death of John XXIII during, 228
  as distinguished by openness from previous councils,
    225
  Dogmatic Constitution on Divine Revelation from, 5,
    150
  family restored as basic unit of Church by, 158–59
  first session of, 228
  fourth session of, 234–35
  liturgy of the Word and liturgy of the Eucharist dis-
    cussed in, 37
  modernist view accepted at, 192, 209
  opening of, 220
  Protestant and Eastern Orthodox Church observers
    at, 220
  response of Church to new world through, 121
  second session of, 230
  synod of bishops started following, 165–66, 234–35
  third session of, 232–33
Sermon on the Mount, 48
Simony, 121
Sloyan, Gerard, 2
Socrates, Council of Ephesus described by, 84, 85
Spanish Inquisition, 115, 146–47
Spellman, Francis, opinion of John XXIII of, 219
Stephen, as first Christian martyr, 22, 24
Storytelling, *xvii*, 44–45

Suenens, Léon-Joseph
    as Second Vatican Council moderator, 231
    focus of Second Vatican Council suggested by, 227
Syllabus of Errors by Pius IX, 175–76, 178

Tardini, Domenico, 223
Tennyson, Alfred Lord, *xiv*
Tertullian, Quintus Septimus Florens, as Montanast,
    33–34
Tetzel, Johannes, promotion of indulgence by, 132–33
Theodoret, two natures of Christ described by, 87
Theodosius, acceptance of Christianity as official religion
    of Roman Empire by, 71
Theodosius II
    Council of Ephesus called by, 83
    death of, 89
    second Council of Ephesus called by, 87
Theological schools, early, 36
Theotokus, as term for Mary, mother of Jesus
    in Chalcedonian doctrine, 93
    debate about, 82, 85, 86
Third Letter of John, relative importance of, 56
Thomas Aquinas
    endorsed for his philosophy by Leo XII, 193–94
    as source of scholastic theology for ultramontanism
        and antimodernism, 173, 201
Tisserant, Eugene, 233–34
Trinity, 81–82

Turro, James, 57

Twelve
   experience of risen Christ by, 20
   history of, 9–10
   as leaders selected by Jesus, 22
   lists of names as representative of twelve tribes of
      Israel for, 22
   persecution of, 24

Tyrrell, George, modernists defined by, 200

Ultramontanism, 165–85
   benefits of, 184–85
   and Cardinal Manning, 180
   connections between antimodernism in 1900s and, 192
   disadvantages of, 185
   opponents of, at First Vatican Council, 178
   Pius IX as supporter of, 170–73
   response to pope's encyclical on, 175–76
   strength in France of, 172, 176

Vatican II. *See* Second Vatican Council (1962–65)

Veneration of saints and relics, 148–49

von Döllinger, John Joseph Ignaz, 175

Vulgate, as translation of Bible approved at Council of
      Trent, 150

Whitehead, Alfred North, *xvi*

Also from

Loyola Press

THE GIFT OF PEACE
Personal Reflections
by Joseph Cardinal Bernardin

"In this gem of a book, reminiscent of the best of Henri Nouwen, Bernardin stresses the importance of regular prayer, the need for loving human relationships and the profound peace that comes from trusting God even in the worst of times."
—Publishers Weekly
ISBN: 0-8294-0955-6; $17.95 hardcover

CONTACT WITH GOD
Retreat Conferences
by Anthony de Mello, S.J.

"De Mello rejected all gimmicks and all jargon, and he had a healthy respect for the classic spiritual writings. No wonder he was so popular and that his books continue to be so influential."
—Praying Magazine
ISBN: 0-8294-0726-X; $10.95 paperback

THE SEEKER'S GUIDE TO BEING CATHOLIC
by Mitch Finley

"All Catholics are 'seekers' so this book is good for all of us. But it is particularly good for marginal Catholics, uneasy Catholics, troubled Catholics, borderline Catholics, ex-Catholics who wonder and worry about their ex ness. It would also be helpful to those who feel attracted to Catholicism, but do not know why."
—Theodore M. Hesburgh, C.S.C., University of Notre Dame President Emeritus
ISBN: 0-8294-0934-3; $10.95 paperback

Available at your local bookstore or order direct from Loyola Press.
Send your check, money order, or VISA/MasterCard information (including
$4.50 for shipping one copy, $5.00 for two copies, or $6.50 for three) to:

LOYOLA PRESS, ATTN: CUSTOMER SERVICE,
3441 NORTH ASHLAND AVENUE, CHICAGO, ILLINOIS 60657
800-621-1008